THE MARTYRDOM OF MAEV & OTHER IRISH STORIES

Harold Frederic

THE MARTYRDOM OF MAEV & OTHER IRISH STORIES

Edited by Jack Morgan

The Catholic University of America Press
Washington, D.C.

Design and typesetting by Kachergis Book Design

Library of Congress Cataloging-in-Publication Data
Frederic, Harold, 1856–1898.
[Short stories. Selections]
The Martyrdom of Maev and other Irish stories / Harold Frederic ;
edited by Jack Morgan.
pages cm
Includes bibliographical references.
ISBN 978-0-8132-2781-8 (pbk. : alk. paper)
1. Ireland—Fiction.   I. Morgan, Jack, 1939– editor.   II. Title.
PS1706.M67 2015
813'.4—dc23   2015016883

To Deborah McWilliams

CONTENTS

Acknowledgments   ix

Introduction by Jack Morgan   xi

PART I

1. The Martyrdom of Maev   3

2. The Lady of Muirisc   47

PART II

3. In the Shadow of Gabriel   71

4. The Path of Murtogh   86

5. The Wooing of Teige   110

6. The Truce of the Bishop   127

Chronology   155

Bibliography   157

ACKNOWLEDGMENTS

Thanks are owed to Trevor Lipscombe, director of the Catholic University Press of America, Theresa Walker, managing editor, and Nicole Wayland, copy editor. I am grateful to the library staffs at Missouri University of Science and Technology, the Library of Congress, University College Dublin, and University College Cork.

I appreciate the assistance of Professor Brian O'Conchubhair, Sue Hill of Mizen Tourism in Goleen, Michael Corbett of Birding Ireland, Kevin O'Callaghan at Ordnance Survey Ireland, and Mizen residents who pointed the way on my walks there. Edward O'Mahony has been especially helpful and generous with his knowledge of Cork and Mizen Peninsula. He also read and commented on the introduction. My colleague, Anne Coterill, read parts of the text and was encouraging from the start of the project.

Claire McVeigh (redrattledesign, St. Albans, UK) kindly granted me permission to use the Mizen (Ivehagh) Peninsula map that appears here, which she customized for this book. The original version of Claire's map appears in Jo Kerrigan and Richard Mills, *West Cork: A Place Apart* (Dublin: O'Brien Press).

Finally, thanks to Greg Delanty for years ago showing me around wonderful Cork City.

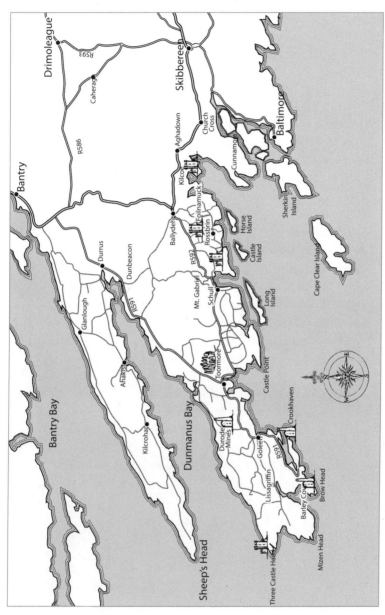

MIZEN (IVEHAGH) PENINSULA

INTRODUCTION

Jack Morgan

Harold Frederic is best known as an American regionalist-realist writer of the nineteenth century associated with northern New York State. This literary profile ignores, however, the exceptional attention he devoted to Irish-American and Irish subject matter—political and literary, contemporary and historical—during two decades of the Irish Revival, from the 1880s until his death in 1898. In the case of his classic American novel *The Damnation of Theron Ware* (1896), set in the Utica, New York, area in the 1870s, his American regionalist involvements and his Irish ones were both in play and brilliantly intertwined; the book stands as the only work in American fiction in which the people of the Irish Famine Diaspora figure prominently aside from *The Irish Stories of Sarah Orne Jewett*. It also stands out in that, as John Henry Raleigh noted in his introduction to a 1967 *Theron Ware* edition, it "shows Irish Catholicism conquering American Protestantism, a happening without parallel in an important American novel."[1] Thomas Ferraro wrote in 2005 regarding *Theron Ware*: "Thanks to Frederic, we ... really are going to have to revise our 'notions of the Irish.'"[2] The novel refuses to remain outside the canon and again and again comes to the fore. Willa Cather at the turn of the century judged its first two hundred pages to be "as good as anything in American litera-

1. John Henry Raleigh, introduction to *The Damnation of Theron Ware* (New York: Holt, 1967), xv.

2. Thomas J. Ferraro, "Of 'Lascivious Mysticism' and Other Hibernian Matters," *U.S. Catholic Historian* 23, no. 3 (Summer 2005): 17.

ture."[3] In 1995, close to the book's centenary, Joyce Carol Oates in a *New York Times* article titled "Rediscovering Harold Frederic" wrote: "WHAT a wonderful novel is *The Damnation of Theron Ware!*"[4]

Frederic's Irish-related work outside of *Theron Ware*, however, work set in Ireland that links him to the Irish Literary Renaissance, has not enjoyed that kind of recognition. Though Frederic was—at the height of his literary skills and the height of the Revival—"writing the Irish West," to borrow Eamonn Wall's book title, his Irish stories have remained virtually unknown. He wrote, and intended to eventually collect in one volume, a series of tales with the west of Ireland as their setting, but his untimely death from a stroke when he was just over forty precluded the fulfillment of that work in progress, and the significant amount of it that he did complete has never before been published except in some magazines of the time. While Frederic was writing these stories of western Ireland, Henry James was preoccupied with Italy, France, and England, as Hawthorne had been, and the American literary imagination continued over time to take these countries as the default definition of "abroad," the expected locales of literary expatriation, while Ireland was overlooked in this regard. As an American expatriate choosing Ireland as a subject, Frederic would be virtually alone in literary history until much later when J. P. Donleavy's *Ginger Man* appeared in 1955. Frederic's Irish works are generally Irish historical, however, more in the mode of Thomas Flanagan's *The Year of the French* (2004).

3. Willa Cather, *The World and the Parish: Willa Cather's Articles and Reviews 1893–1902*, vol. 2, ed. William M. Curtin (Lincoln: University of Nebraska Press, 1970), 711.

4. Joyce Carol Oates, "Rediscovering Harold Frederic," *New York Times Book Review*, December 17, 1995, 24. Regarding the fortunes of Frederic's literary reputation over time, see Glenn D. Klopfenstein, "'The Flying Dutchman of American Literature': Harold Frederic and the American Canon, a Centenary Overview," *American Literary Realism* 30, no. 1 (1997): 34–46.

INTRODUCTION

A former editor of the *Utica Daily Observer* and later the *Albany Evening Journal*, Frederic was an upstate New Yorker of German Methodist upbringing, making it a perhaps unlikely outcome that so much of his attention would be turned in time to things Irish. He had published only two New York novels, both in 1890, before publishing a rather eccentric Irish romance, *The Return of the O'Mahony*, in 1892. Even his New York state works such as *Seth's Brother's Wife*, *The Lawton Girl*, *The Copperhead*, and *Theron Ware* owed, as Frederic himself declared, something to an Irish example—that of his friend T. P. O'Connor's story "Dead Man's Island" serialized in the *Weekly Echo* in 1885 and informed by the Cork localism O'Connor was conversant with from boyhood.[5] Impressed with Frederic's New York writing, and regarding it as a major step forward in American realism, Stephen Crane was for a while concerned about Frederic's choice of other subjects following upon his appointment as London correspondent for the *New York Times* in 1884. When he eventually met Frederic for the first time, in 1897, Crane had been concerned beforehand that Frederic might have become Europeanized in manner and mind given his residence in England, but his worries proved unfounded: "There was a tall, heavy man, mustached and straight-glanced, seated in a leather chair in the smoking room of a club, telling a story to a circle of intent people with all the skill of one trained in an American newspaper school. At a distance he might have been even then the editor of the Albany *Journal*.... Frederic was to be to me a cosmopolitan figure, repre-

5. Bridget Bennett, *The Damnation of Harold Frederic: His Lives and Works* (Syracuse, N.Y.: Syracuse University Press, 1997), 145. "Dead Man's Island" also appeared in the January-February issues of the Boston Catholic monthly *Donahoe's Magazine* in 1856. Though the O'Connor story, or novella, was a modest literary piece, its influence can be seen in Frederic's "The Martyrdom of Maev" especially. O'Connor broached something in his story that is relevant to the grim drama inscribed in "The Martyrdom of Maev": he remarked that in the Ireland of the time, especially rural Ireland, the fate of a girl who had "fallen" was dire, the society merciless.

senting many ways and many peoples; and, behold, he was still
the familiar figure, with no gilding or varnish, a great reminis-
cent panorama of the Mohawk Valley."

The cosmopolitan range of Frederic's work to which Crane
refers included by that time *The New Exodus: A Study of Israel in
Russia* (1892) and novels *Gloria Mundi* (1898) and *The Market Place*
(1899) set in England and then under way, as well as his earlier
intrepid coverage of the cholera epidemic in France in the summer of 1884 during which he traveled to the most disease-ridden
areas, his reports being widely hailed as courageous, exemplary journalism. A *New York Star* editorial in August of that year
judged that Frederic's epidemic articles placed him "among
the few great newspaper correspondents of the age."[6] Crane remarked, however, that Frederic's expatriation and journalistic
fame had not affected his powers as a novelist and short-story
writer. Contemporaneously with his European reportage, Crane
notes, "There was Frederic doing his locality, doing his Mohawk
valley, with the strong trained hand of a great craftsman." Noting in the same essay the precision of Frederic's grasp of English
life, Crane added that it was "only equaled by the precision with
which he has grasped Irish life."[7]

After Frederic's move to England in 1884, Ireland lay close
by, and the island charmed him as had the new Irish arrivals
he encountered in his native Utica, New York, in the 1870s, with
the result that he became increasingly a hibernophile. Moving
between London and Ireland as Yeats did, Frederic was a mem-
ber of the Irish Literary Society in Dublin and the London Irish
Literary Society, whose membership included Yeats, George
Bernard Shaw, Conon Doyle, Bram Stoker, and Douglas Hyde,

6. A *New York Times* report on July 31, 1884, reprinted this *New York Star*
editorial and similar ones praising Frederic's coverage of the epidemic, such as
one from the *Troy Times* headlined "A Great Service to Humanity."

7. Stephen Crane, "Harold Frederic," in *Crane: Prose and Poetry* (New York:
Library of America, 1996), 984, 987.

among others.[8] Frederic's preoccupations became those prevalent in Revivalist Ireland: Irish nationalism, the country's tragic historical narrative, the newly energized Gaelic antiquarian research, and the survival of traditional culture in the West. The Americanist Stanton Garner observed that "of all the aspects of Harold Frederic's multifaceted life and character his fascination with Ireland and the Irish people is among the most obscure."[9]

Touring the country with T. P. O'Connor and Timothy Healy, having dinner with Parnell at the latter's Wicklow home, and having Parnell to dinner at his own home, Frederic became an increasingly informed student of Irish nationalist politics and a dedicated advocate for Irish independence during the Gladstone/Parnell era.[10] In *Ireland in the New Century* (1904), Horace Plunkett recalled a conversation with Frederic shortly before the latter's death. "He told me that the 'Irish Question' possessed for him a fascination for which he could give no rational explanation."[11]

On a return trip to Utica in 1886, speaking before an Irish National League convention, Frederic affirmed his unreserved identification with the Irish cause:

He pointed out that America usually only receives the English point of view and that the Irish immigrants to America are of the poorest classes, so he had originally believed that "there was something to

---

8. Stanton Garner, "Some Notes on Harold Frederic in Ireland," *American Literature* 39, no. 1 (March 1967): 67–68. Given the small space and insularity of Ireland, it is not unlikely that in his research Frederic may have encountered Canon John O'Mahony, who was presumably studying the same material at the same time, though his *History of the O'Mahony Septs of Kinelmeky and Iveagh* did not begin to appear in print until 1906, after Frederic's death.

9. Garner, "Some Notes on Harold Frederic in Ireland," 60. Frederic introduced Crane and his wife, Cora, to Ireland as well, and Crane would spend the last year of his life at work on an Irish romance, *The O'Ruddy*, continuing to work on it on his death bed.

10. Robert M. Myers, *Reluctant Expatriate: The Life of Harold Frederic* (Westport, Conn.: Greenwood, 1995), 51.

11. Horace Plunkett, *Ireland in the New Century* (London: J. Murray, 1904), 161.

the English side of the case." However, during his trip to Ireland he saw a land "where rogues put the law on honest men, where no one but the crows and the tax gatherer have enough to eat, and then [he] came back an Irishman." He explained that if his newsletters seemed biased, it was because "there is no cool, dispassionate, half-way house between right and wrong, between decency and outrage." So enthusiastic was Frederic in his support for Ireland that Parnell and Healy even discussed the unlikely possibility of sending him to Parliament to represent an Irish borough.[12]

Frank Harris, on the occasion of Frederic's death in 1898, wrote that Frederic's desire to work for the *New York Times* out of London "sprang first from his passionate belief in the justice of the Irish cause" and that during Frederic's tenure there "it is not too much to say that the *New York Times* ... did more to arouse American sympathy with Ireland ... than any other journal."[13] That tenure was not a happy one, however, and from the start the *Times* editor was not pleased with what he perceived as an Irish fixation in Frederic's dispatches; the newspaper had to be dragged along, and Frederick was subject to constant admonishment for his Irish interests. He had to justify his reportage at every turn, writing, for example, to the *Times* editor, Charles R. Miller, from London: "I have got the inside of everything Irish here and in Dublin.... I assume you will regard this as advantageous." And on another occasion: "The Irish are a clannish people—and a great reading people. I may be wrong, but I should think such a clientele would be worth cultivating, not in the least by pandering, but by courteous and sympathetic comment." Miller's resistance persisted, however, as evidenced by an angry letter in 1893 regarding what he saw as excessive coverage of the Home Rule issue. Miller asserted that there was not that wide an American interest in the matter: "I have often

12. Myers, *Reluctant Expatriate*, 51.
13. Frank Harris, "Harold Frederic Ad Memoriam," *Saturday Review of Politics, Literature, Science, and Art* LXXXVI, no. 527 (October 22, 1898): 527.

told you that I wanted you to give a greater variety of news interest to your cables, and you have never been able or seen fit to comply with my directions. I expect you to do so."[14] It may only have been for the stature Frederic's cholera epidemic coverage of 1884 had brought him that he was able to weather the attempts at editorial censorship and write, for example, an article in 1885 on the death of Irish Cardinal McCabe in which he articulated Irish nationalist concern regarding pressure that Britain might bring to bear on the choice of McCabe's successor. "The result to the morale of the Church in Ireland is likely to be most sinister," he warned, "if England should be allowed to name the man, as she has been in the past."[15]

In 1895 Frederic wrote to John Nicol Dunn, editor of the British weekly *Black and White*, that he hoped to complete seven or eight Irish stories relating to castle fortresses of the O'Mahony sept in West Cork, "ranging in point of time from 1170 to 1602." The stories would especially involve the O'Mahony clan of West Carbery, specifically of the Ivehagh Peninsula[16] (Mizen Head), which lies with the Beara Peninsula, Bantry Bay, the Sheep's Head Peninsula, and Dunmanus Bay to its west-northwest, and with Roaring Water Bay to its east. "I have been toiling for years on the archeology of [the O'Mahony] district and family," he informed Dunn, "and when the stories are all written and made

14. Frederic to Miller, September 23, 1884; September 4, 1885. Miller to Frederic, September 8, 1893. Quoted in Myers, *Reluctant Expatriate*, 51, 53, 117.

15. Harold Frederic, "London's Budget of News," *New York Times*, February 15, 1885, 1. British Government displeasure with Frederic being the *Times* correspondent in London, and with his pro-Irish reportage, must have been great indeed, and he must have been carefully watched. When Frederic was given a dinner at Delmonico's in New York prior to his return to England following a U.S. visit in 1886, prominently in attendance was General Carroll-Tevis, a longtime British spy working in Irish nationalist circles ("Dinner to Mr. Harold Frederic," *New York Times*, June 29, 1886). Regarding Tevis as a British agent, see Christy Campbell, *Fenian Fire* (New York: Harper, 2003).

16. The Ivehagh Peninsula not to be confused with the *Iveragh* Peninsula in Kerry.

into a book, I fancy the work will be unique in more ways than one."[17] The present book brings together four stories, set toward the end of Gaelic Ireland, that Frederic finished and published in magazines in 1895–96 and two of his stories set in the west of Ireland in the second half of the nineteenth century.[18]

The two nineteenth-century stories are "The Martyrdom of Maev" and "The Lady of Muirisc," the latter of which has represented some problems for Frederic scholarship. He recorded in his pocket diary on October 16, 1891, that he had completed a story titled "The Lady of Muirisc," but no such work ever appeared in magazine publication, nor is it to be found among Frederic's papers at the Library of Congress. A year after the mention of the story in his notebook, however, Frederic published the novel *The Return of the O'Mahony*, which includes a long episode titled "The Lady of Muirisc." The present editor's assumption is that Frederic wrote the piece first as a short story and then decided to build the novel around it, or, having written it as part of the novel, recognized its possibilities as a separate narrative. Supportive of this conclusion is the fact that the episode in the novel in which Kate meets her American cousin—who unbeknownst to her or him is the heir to the local, very derelict, O'Mahony estate—is of a tenor strangely at odds with the peculiar, virtually screwball comic work that surrounds it, a picaresque romp of a novel so complex in its whirling unfoldment that, though not without its merits, it never gained any audience to speak of. That narrative moves, with seemingly wild abandonment, from F Company in the Union Army in the American Civil war to the ludicrous

17. Harold Frederic, "Letter to James N. Dunn," in *The Correspondence of Harold Frederic*. The Harold Frederic Edition, vol. 1 (Fort Worth: Texas Christian University Press, 1977), 392.

18. Though the time frame of the tales involves years that would not usually be designated "medieval" but "early modern," the world of the far western coast of Ireland in the late 1500s can surely be so designated—therefore in this introduction "medieval" is sometimes used to refer to Frederic's historical stories.

convent of the unaffiliated—though the "nuns" don't know it—
"Order of the Hostage's Tears" in a bizarre, isolated village in
Cork. The "Lady of Muirisc" episode in the book, however, involving Kate O'Mahony, is of a quiet, plaintiff, and serious character,
oddly situated in the context of an otherwise rough-hewn work.
Furthermore, by the early 1890s Frederic had two families
to support—one within wedlock, the other not—and was financially strapped; it was his practice to publish the same work in
as many venues as possible. "The Wooing of Teige," for example,
was published in both *The Pall Mall Magazine* and *Little's Living
Age* in the same year. "In the Shadow of Gabriel" was similarly
double-published, appearing almost simultaneously in *The
New York Ledger* and, in England, in *Black and White*. He was not
one, that is, to have a completed story on hand and not see to
its publication forthwith. It would seem, as noted, that he wrote
"The Lady of Muirisc" and decided to fit the story into a novel
recently begun—a novel being more remunerative anyway. In
the end, the story, as noted, sits uncomfortably in *The Return*,
arguably bespeaking its independent origin. "The Lady of Muirisc" is published here, therefore, as an independent work, one
which complements the four historical O'Mahony tales in that
it portrays the clan some two hundred and fifty years later, in
the same landscape, and concludes on Mount Gabriel where the
first of the medieval narratives begins.[19] This presentation has
required some editing—breaks in the episode have been elimi-
nated, and occasional remarks by the narrator or characters
that would reference elements of the novel's plot have been de-
leted and the deletions marked by bracketed ellipses.
"The Lady of Muirisc" takes place in the parish of Kilmoe at

19. This seems more likely than Garner's supposition of a distinct "missing" tale, which would suppose Frederic titled two separate pieces "The Lady
of Muirisc" within months of each other and would leave unexplained how a
completed tale would go missing—never, as noted, to appear in a magazine or
be accounted for in his papers.

the southern tip of the Ivehagh Peninsula, the area that inspired Frederic's series of what Garner described as "haunting tales of the O'Mahony septs, which, despite their small bulk, relate him to the Irish literary Renaissance."[20] While representing a unique American literary presence in the Ireland of the Revival, however, Frederic did not yield to the unreserved Irish romanticism around at the time; like most things in his life, his Irish preoccupation, while often enthusiastic, was of a cautious, skeptical kind that would mark him as arguably more Joycean than Yeatsean and more a Revival fellow traveler than an affiliate. He did greatly relish Ireland, however, especially the stark remoteness of the western Cork coast, which he described in a manner reflecting his sense of the place as quasi-gothic, a mood that sometimes comes to the fore in his coastal stories: "It is an ancient and sterile and storm-beaten parish, this Kilmoe, thrust out in expiation of some forgotten sin or other to exist beyond the pale of human companionship. Its sons and daughters, scattered in tiny, isolated hamlets over its barren area, hear never a stranger's voice—and their own speech is slow and low of tone because the real right to make a noise there belongs to the shrieking gulls and the wild, west wind and the towering, foam-fanged waves, which dash themselves, in tireless rivalry with the thunder, against its cliffs."[21] Both nineteenth-century stories portray the modern reverberations of a tragic historical period—the Elizabethan era in which Frederic's historical narratives take place. "The Martyrdom of Maev," occurs in the context of the evictions, confiscations, and famine still defining Irish life in the second half of the nineteenth century, long after the outrages of the sixteenth century that frame the four earlier stories, and after the passing of Ascendancy Ireland. It is now a country where

20. Stanton Garner, *Harold Frederic* (Minneapolis: University of Minnesota Press, 1969), 30.

21. Harold Frederic, *The Return of the O'Mahony* (New York: Bonner's Sons, 1892), 167.

the common people are dominated by merchants and officials, the Royal Constabulary, and absentee landlords and their callous local agents. The Maev story occurs not in South Munster but farther west, in Connacht, in the early 1880s, and had, when Frederic wrote Dunn about his Irish stories, already been published in the *New York Ledger* in 1890. Of the medieval stories, "In the Shadow of Gabriel" appeared in *Black and White*, "The Truce of the Bishop" in *Yellow Book*, and "The Path of Murtogh" in *The Idler*, all in 1895. "The Wooing of Teige" appeared in *Pall Mall Magazine* in 1896. The present text adheres to these magazine versions, no later revisions having been made by Frederic. A few egregious typographical errors have been addressed, and, for the sake of uniformity and readability, some punctuation eccentricities—perhaps owing to different editors—have been adjusted.

The historical tales begin in 1550 near Mount Gabriel, where "The Lady of Muirisc" concludes, overlooking the seas of West Cork. Turlogh has lately inherited the chieftainship of Dunbeekin. This story and "The Truce of the Bishop," both of which are about Turlogh, frame the sixteenth-century narratives. Lost sight of after Frederic's early death, however, the stories in question were overlooked or ignored even by Frederic scholars and go unmentioned as late as Hoyt C. Franchere and Thomas F. O'Donnell's *Harold Frederic* (1961). A 1967 article by Stanton Garner in *American Literature*, however, called attention to these works for which Frederic had had high hopes. "The riches of these tales are quite unexpected," Garner writes. Far from viewing them as an anomalous and lesser aspect of Frederic's work, he characterizes them as serious in intent, "mature works of a mature artist," and remarks their "grace and poetry."[22] Two years later, in 1969, in a Harold Frederic number in the University of Minnesota pamphlet series on American writers, Garner devoted two pages to the stories, and his evaluation was again

---

22. Garner, "Some Notes on Harold Frederic in Ireland," 68, 72.

very positive. He saw "The Truce of the Bishop," for example, the elegiac concluding story in the present book, as representing the impressive fruition of half a decade of the author's literary development: "at precisely this point Frederic's period of consolidation ended, his literary maturity complete." The stories "reveal Frederic at a new plateau of achievement," writes Garner, "in full command of a supple style which ranges from lush lyricism to sparse tragedy."[23] "The Path of Murtogh" is a powerful tour de force of horror that Frederic himself judged to be "by far the strongest thing I have ever done."[24] The year after it and "The Truth of the Bishop" were published, his refined narrative skills would be manifested in novelistic form in *The Damnation of Theron Ware*. His narrative talents were evident even earlier, however, in works published in the early nineties, including "The Martyrdom of Maev," a story that captures vividly the atmosphere of the extraordinarily dark years in western Ireland around 1879–85.

When these Irish tales appeared, especially the sixteenth-century ones, contemporary critics must have been puzzled and may have assumed that as London correspondent for the *Times*, traveling a good deal in Ireland, he had been caught up in the Celtic mystique then in vogue. But granted some Revival bearing on them, they are a thing unto themselves; they do not indulge in the soulful Celtic nostalgia that often characterizes Irish historical fiction. If Frederic's earlier American historical fiction was "important for emancipating the genre from the romantic themes which still pervaded it," these stories might be said to do the same for Irish historical fiction as then practiced, bringing a realist and even naturalist sensibility to the genre.[25] Not overlooked in them, for instance, is the

23. Garner, *Harold Frederic*, 30–31.
24. Frederic, "Letter to James N. Dunn," 391.
25. Robert H. Woodward, "Harold Frederic: A Study of his Novels, Short Stories, and Plays" (doctoral dissertation), Bloomington, Indiana University, 1957, 1.

general savagery of the times, including the appalling sacks of one Irish clan by another. The clans were far from harmonious, and English strategy took advantage of that. When in 1565, for example, in order to sow discord in Munster, two Irish chieftains were summoned to London and forced to surrender their land and have it newly granted to them by the Crown, the discordant effects London intended came about.[26] The sixteenth-century violence among clans is chillingly suggested in "The Path of Murtogh" when Murtogh's faithful bard recalls how his eyes were put out in a raid when he was a child: "I was in my mother's arms. There were men breaking in through the wall, and the kine bellowing outside, and my father cut down; and then it was like my mother drew her cloak tight over my head,—and no one ever came to take it off again." The young priest in the same story is prematurely grey, owing, apparently, to the horror he witnessed when Murtogh sacked his, the priest's, father's settlement.

Frederic's interest in West Cork, Mount Gabriel, the ruins at Dunlough, and the history of the O'Mahonys reflected the time he spent in the area of Dunmanus Bay with his mistress Kate Lyon, whose mother was an O'Mahony (as was Celia Madden's mother in *The Damnation of Theron Ware*).[27] He began to focus on the area of the Ivehagh Peninsula, where O'Mahony chiefs reigned in the sixteenth century, west of O'Driscoll territory, within the broader lordship of McCarthy Reagh. The coast there, still barely discovered when he visited, with its "wild mountain paths and tempest-lashed fiords," captured his imagination. In her story "The Deluge at Nordeney," Isak Dinesen remarks that it was not until the first quarter of the nineteenth century that a new aesthetic noting the sublimity of bleak, stormy, coastal

26. Edward O'Mahony, "West Cork and the Elizabethan Wars 1565–1603," http://www.geocities.ws/eomahon?Elizabeathan.htm.

27. Celia was identified as an O'Mahony at least in Frederic's preliminary notes for the novel (see Stanton Garner's "Note on the Text" introduction to the University of Nebraska Press edition of *Theron Ware*, 1985).

landscapes began to take hold widely—even in North Atlantic countries where formerly the sea had been regarded as cruel, a threatening maelstrom. Even in Yeats's poem "A Prayer for my Daughter," a dark impression of the sea and its "murderous innocence" survives.[28] This older sense of the sea may account for, as Frederic noted, the striking beauty of the coast at Dunmanus going for so long undiscovered.[29] The Atlantic shores of Ireland in his sixteenth-century stories are mostly in the preromantic vein; this is especially notable in the "Path of Murtogh," in which sinister currents "writhe" below the high cliffs. As in Synge's *Riders to the Sea* or Robert Flaherty's film *Man of Aran*, the ocean is here portrayed as nihilistic—more cruel than benign. Frederic's personal sense of the contemporary Irish seascape, however, was the modern one Dinesen describes wherein the sea's very starkness situates an elemental beauty. "If such another combination of mountain scenery, savage abyss of sea wall, and vast expanse of open ocean existed elsewhere in Northern Europe," he writes of the west Cork coast as late as the 1890s, "the guide books would be full of it, and the intelligent tourist would know it all by heart. Being in Ireland, I know of no one but myself and an artist-companion, outside the class of native peasantry, who has ever seen it."[30]

His interest in Ireland in general, however, had commenced earlier, as mentioned, in Utica, New York, in the 1870s, at which time he was in his late teens and employed by the *Utica Daily Observer*. The town had a large Irish population by then, the influx of immigrants having begun during the Erie Canal construction in the 1820s. Though a product of the town's older,

28. William Butler Yeats, *The Collected Poems of William Butler Yeats*, ed. Richard J. Finneran (New York: Collier, 1989), 188–90.

29. Isak Dinesen, "The Deluge at Nordeney," in *Seven Gothic Tales* (New York: Vintage: 1991), 1.

30. Harold Frederic, "The Coast of White Foam," *New York Times Magazine*, November 1, 1896, 4.

German community, Frederic took to the new arrivals. The Irish love of talk, beer, politics, newspapers, and festivity apparently contrasted dramatically with the comparatively dour Methodist milieu he had previously known—he himself had a reputation as an enthusiastic conversationalist and bon vivant. He made many friends among the Irish, including a close friendship with the Irish-born and Irish nationalist Father Edward A. Terry, pastor of St. John's Church in Utica. There began then a captivation with these Irish strangers and their country that would become a defining aspect of Frederic's life. At an Irish banquet in the town, a speaker had once hailed the Erie Canal as "a capital road from Cork to Utica."[31] Ironically enough, Frederic traveled the other way—from Utica to Cork.

His interest in the Irish political affairs of the 1880s and 1890s brought him into an especially close association with MP Timothy Healy. A lawyer from West Cork and a journalist, writer, and talented orator, Healy was instrumental in Parnell's rise to power and was himself a passionate and skilled advocate for land reform and on behalf of Irish victims of eviction and jailed Irish political prisoners. During the devastating crop failures of the 1870s, when tenants saw their rents triple, he was arrested as a land-reform agitator for his aggressive championing of the cause of a Bantry family who were driven to living under a rowboat after eviction from their home.[32] This incident became an important element in "The Martyrdom of Maev," which is set in the same time period and in which Mitchel Daunt's parents have to resort to living beneath an inverted boat, leading to Mitchel's mother's death and his father's losing his mind.

His friendship with Healy, and political like-mindedness, would lead to unpleasant complications for Frederic, however,

31. Quoted in Allen G. Noble, *An Ethnic Geography of Utica, New York* (Lewiston, N.Y.: The Edwin Mellen Press, 1999).

32. Frank Callanan, *T. M. Healy* (Cork: Cork University Press, 1996), 44.

when in the scandal of 1890–91 Healy broke with Parnell, becoming the major anti-Parnellite MP and vehemently leading the anti-Parnell initiatives that destroyed the Irish leader and the advances toward home rule for which he was responsible. To many, Healy became the face of betrayal; Liam O'Flaherty wrote that for a time Healy was the most unpopular man in Ireland.[33] Frank Callanan notes regarding James Joyce, a devoted Parnellite, that from his poem "Et Tu Healy," written at the age of nine, to *Finnegans Wake*, "Healy pervades Joyce's disconsolate aftermath of Parnell, exuding a sanctimonious villainy."[34] Frederic inevitably suffered for his association with the Healyite circle, an association that in the end placed him on what most perceived to be the wrong side of contemporary Irish history. His *Times* reportage had often supported Healy's positions and the latter's growing estrangement from Parnell; even Frederic's reports on the occasion of Parnell's death were harsh and unsympathetic. This was the beginning of that long period during which it seemed, as Frank O'Connor described it, that "the intellect of Ireland had been driven into the wilderness,"[35] and men woefully inferior to Parnell came upon the scene. Not until 1893, by which time the consequences of Parnell's fall were becoming ever more manifest, did Frederic write of Parnell, though begrudgingly, in comparatively positive terms, describing him as "that sad, shadowy figure, prophet, desperado, ruler, charlatan, madman, martyr all in one—the last commanding personality in hapless Ireland's history."[36] Healy long outlived Frederic and to some extent outlived the odium that came with his abandonment of Parnell, becoming the first governor-general of the Irish Free State in 1922. Frederic had died years previous, how-

33. Liam O'Flaherty, *The Life of Tim Healy* (New York: Harcourt, 1927).

34. Callanan, *T. M. Healy*, xxiv.

35. Frank O'Connor, *The Big Fellow* (Dublin: Poolbeg, [1937] 1979), 16.

36. Harold Frederic, "The Ireland of Today," *Fortnightly Review* LX (November 1893): 705.

ever, when Irish nationalist aspirations, in the 1890s, were faring badly, and in his last years his Irish interests were expressed in more literary and less political terms.

He wrote a farewell of sorts to Irish politics in 1893—a long, detailed, and pessimistic profile titled "The Ireland of Today." This was the year in which the Second Home Rule bill failed and the realization of the loss of Parnell was spreading an ever wider gloom in the land. In the essay, published anonymously in the *Fortnightly Review*, Frederic gave vent to his own frustration with what he saw as a neurotic strain in Irish life—far too much speechifying, too great a glorification of heroes, and too little application of energies to addressing contemporary issues in a practical way. In another essay in the same journal that year ("The Rhetoricians of Ireland"), he again expressed concern regarding traditional Irish overindulgences, noting the excessive Irish fondness for rhetoric, an issue he touched upon yet again in a *New York Times* piece in 1896, in which he saw this bent epitomized in the often-quixotic fictions and fulsome solicitude of the traditional Irish bards.[37] He had in mind perhaps less the ancient Gaelic *filii* who was integral to the culture and whose verses held and preserved the ethos of the tribe and more the bard in an era of decline who peddled inflated historical narratives and "always had a wealth of blarneying adjectives at the tip of his goose quill."[38] Frederic felt that the nineteenth-century record in Irish history, one of political high-emotionalism and febrile debate, likewise obscured the reality "that all the while there was existing in Ireland a population of intelligent human beings possessing average skulls and in ordinary affairs as sane and sensible as oth-

37. Harold Frederic, "The Rhetoricians of Ireland," *Fortnightly Review* 60 (December 1, 1893): 713–27; "The Coast of White Foam," 4–5.

38. Frederic, "The Coast of White Foam," 4. This point of view was, of course, not unique to Frederic; it has been widely articulated in Irish literature. It would be, for instance, Sean O'Casey's view as well and would lie at the bitter heart of his *Juno and the Paycock* (1924).

er people."[39] His antirhetorical and antiromantic bent bears upon some of the stories in the present collection and finds expression most directly perhaps in "The Wooing of Teige," in which the calm, sensible intelligence of Hugh O'Sullivan stands in contrast to the nonsense spouted tirelessly by the itinerant minstrel Tiarnan *Bladair*. The Teige tale, like the first Turlogh story, deals with the assumption of chieftainship by a young man and the undertaking of an adventure. Teige does not lack for the requisite boldness of a chief but is at first prone to fantasy and faulty judgment, notable in his paying attention to the dreamy bard who leads him on a misguided, though in the end fortunate, journey. His settling into a new realism and maturity by way of Hugh O'Sullivan's example suggests an improved readiness for leadership on his part.

Yeats identified "four bells" that tolled "four deep and tragic notes in Irish history." The first tolling involved the Irish battle against Elizabethan rule at the end of the sixteenth century, culminating in the flight of the Earls when, after decades of warfare, the Irish lost the upper hand at Kinsale—"Here Celtic alternative order/fought, died, 1601," writes Desmond O'Grady.[40] Four of Frederic's Irish tales are set in this tragic era in Munster, the Ivehagh Peninsula previously referred to. The period the stories cover is less than the 1170 to 1602 he had originally planned, however, rather they occur within the chieftainship of Turlogh, running from Christmas day 1550—when "In the Shadow of Gabriel" takes place—to around 1602, years that take in the Elizabethan occupations when English policy in Ireland assumed a deliberate coherence and ruthless determination that contrasted with the less effectual British efforts of earlier decades. Now a thriving vacation

39. Frederic, "The Rhetoricians of Ireland," 714.

40. William Butler Yeats, commentary on his poem "Parnell's Funeral," in *A New Commentary on the Poems of William Butler Yeats*, ed. A. N. Jeffares (London: Macmillan, 1984), 333. Desmond O'Grady, "Kinsale," in *Salmon—A Journey in Poetry: 1981–2007*, ed. Jesse Lenndene (Clare: Salmon, 2008), 313.

area, the Cork coast west from Baltimore to Bantry Bay was then, and even into the nineteenth century, an exceptionally remote region, though not without its resources. Until the last decades of the sixteenth century, the O'Mahonys and other coastal clans had prospered thanks to the region's isolated shores with their forbidding cliffs and shadowy, hidden inlets. There were good pastures, and the area's rich fishing grounds, where herring were abundant, were a particular source of wealth—foreign fishing ships were charged dues, and the clans profited from providing harbor and supplies to these vessels and haven to pirate ships. In O'Mahony territory, Dunlogher—where "The Path of Murtogh" is set—and Leamcon were especially notorious pirate haunts. Adrian Tinniswood describes Leamcon as, in the seventeenth century, more a frontier town than an Irish village.[41] The salvaging, at least as legend would have it, did not always wait for an unfortunate accident. Frederic writes,

Whenever a stormy, wind-swept night set in, the men of Kilmoe tied a lighted lantern on the neck of a cow, and drove the animal to walk along the strand underneath the sea-cliffs. This light, rising and sinking with the movements of the cow, bore a quaint and interesting resemblance to the undulations of an illuminated buoy or boat, rocked on gentle waves; and strange seafaring crafts bent their course in confidence toward it, until they were undeceived. Then the men of Kilmoe would sally forth, riding the tumbling breakers with great bravery and address, in their boats of withes and stretched skin, and enter into possession of all the stranger's goods and chattels.[42]

41. Adrian Tinniswood, *Pirates of Barbary: Corsairs, Conquests, and Captivity in the 17th-Century Mediterranean* (New York: Penguin, 2010). Frederic notes that Elizabethan records mention Dunlogher as a notorious pirate lair ("The Coast of White Foam," 4). Munster's wealth of natural resources is described by the British colonist Robert Payne in *A Brief Description of Ireland* (London, 1590). Payne notes Munster's fertile soil, abundant wild fowl, good livestock, and coastline rich in shellfish. Quoted in Peter Berresford Ellis, *Eyewitness to Irish History* (Hoboken, N.J.: Wiley, 2004), 63–64.

42. Frederic, *The Return of the O'Mahony*, 168.

The days when the O'Mahonys could prosper in their detached coastal villages were numbered, however. With the failure of the Irish resistance to English inroads at the turn of the century, even the secluded O'Mahony settlements fell victim to the foreign incursions sweeping across Munster generally.

If the designation "Elizabethan," at least in Anglo-centric historiography, conjures up associations of newfound sociopolitical dynamism in England, nascent empire, and high literary and scientific achievement, that time frame carries less pleasant connotations in Irish history, something reflected in Frederic's stories. Nothing like tolerance or enlightenment marked the British presence there. *Usnea*, moss from the skulls of corpses, was a significant element in the pharmacopeia of the time, for example, and Francis Bacon, citing possible sources of this highly prized medicinal moss, noted that "heaps of slain bodies" lay available, unburied, in Ireland. During this period, Richard Sugg notes, the corpses piling up throughout the Irish countryside were sought after for the skull trade in England and abroad. In 1566 Humphrey Gilbert was dispatched to Ireland to aide Sir Henry Sidney in the British military campaign. Thomas Churchyard, who served under Gilbert, left a particularly memorable account of Gilbert's dealings with the Irish. He told of how Gilbert ordered "that the heads of all those that were killed in the day, should be cut off from their bodies, and brought to the place where he incamped at night." There, they were "laid on the ground, by each side of the way leading into his own tent: so that none could come into his tent for any cause, but ... he must pass through a lane of heads."[43]

The particularly merciless devastation of Munster in the late 1590s is famously, or infamously, described in Edmund Spenser's *A View of the Present State of Ireland*, wherein Irenius notes with some admiration the efficacy of the agricultural havoc visited

---

43. Richard Sugg, *Mummies, Cannibals, and Vampires: The History of Corpse Medicine from the Renaissance to the Victorians* (New York: Routledge, 2011), 103.

on the Irish population in the 1570s—famine's strategic superiority even to military assault:

Although there should none of them fall by the sword, nor bee slaine by the souldiour, yet thus being kept from manurance, and their cattle from running abroad, by this hard restraint they would quickly consume themselves, and devoure one another. The proof whereof I saw sufficiently exampled in these late warres of Mounster; for, notwithstanding that the same was a most rich and plentifull countrey, full of corn and cattle, that you would have thought they should have beene able to stand long, yet ere one yeare and a halfe they were brought to such wretchednesse as that any stony heart would have rued the same. Out of every corner of the woods and glunnes they came creeping forth upon their hands, for their legges could not beare them; they looked like anatomies of death, they spake like ghosts crying out of their graves.[44]

This terrorism and the following dispossession and plantation campaign—on a scale heretofore unheard of—wounded Ireland grievously. A traumatized country went forward in a crippled state to which it would be bound for centuries. When Brother Dunstan in Frederic's "The Martyrdom of Maev" arrives in Connacht a little less than three hundred years later, he encounters a still-stunned land and people policed by constables with rifles slung over their shoulders: "The rude and somber scenery; the cold sky piled with clouds, pushed glowering landward by Atlantic winds; the wide wastes of barren mountain land ... roofless cabins whose owners had been turned into the ditch only last year; the unspeakable raggedness of the children we passed and who raced madly after us for alms; the indescribable look of woe in the faces of the peasants; the squalor and gloom and hopelessness of it all—I grow sad now as I recall it." Both Frederic's sixteenth-century tales and the modern ones are informed by this

44. Edmund Spenser, *A View of the Present State of Ireland*, ed. Andrew Hadfield and Willy Maley (London: Blackwell, 1997), 101–02.

sense of the shock and sorrow that descended upon Ireland with
the Tudor occupations that were a prelude to Cromwell's later
merciless march across the island—a trauma that entered the
marrow of Irish history and culture. "The Truce of the Bishop"
opens upon a scorched-earth landscape that knows neither harvest nor sewing, the huts are without thatch and abandoned. "It
was the desolation of conquest. The conquered were dead, or in
hiding among the hills. The spoilers, their havoc wrought, had
turned and gone away, with famine spreading wave-like at their
heels." The reverberations of that trauma echo in "The Lady of
Muirisc," as well, set, as noted, around 1877. Kate, having climbed
to the summit of Mount Gabriel and looked out over the land, is
overcome by a dark epiphany: "'Twas, like dreaming," she says,
"and a strange thought came to me: … that this lovely Ireland I
looked down upon was beautiful with the beauty of death; that
'twas the corpse of me country I was taking a last view of."

Kate O'Mahony is twenty-two years old and, in this region
given to fantasy, is "a very lovely and complete reality."[45] She is
climbing to the heights of Mount Gabriel with old Murphy, a
friend-relative and perhaps something of a chaperone—at least
he thinks so—as she is soon perforce to take a nun's veil, and
this may be a last climb in the open spaces and awesome beauty
of the heights near her village from which perspective the ruins
of the castle at Dunlogher can be seen. Kate and old Murphy are
walking toward a lake circled by rushes when they encounter
a heron that flies up and slowly away toward the cliffs and the
sea. A young man at the edge of the lake has a rifle sighted on
the heron, and Kate's alarmed cry saves its life. There is an un-
mistakable reference here to Sarah Orne Jewett's story "A White
Heron," an apt reference since Kate, like Sylvia in Jewett's tale,
is poised on the edge of womanhood, beginning to discover the
greater world beyond her rural home, when she meets a young

45. Frederic, *The Return of the O'Mahony*, 171.

man. The young man in Kate's case is Bernard O'Mahony of Houghton County, Michigan—as mentioned, a distant cousin of hers. A mining engineer, he is prospecting in the area for a company and visiting the local castles as well. He knows his father was from this part of Cork but is unaware that he is himself *the* O'Mahony heir to clan land there.

As noted, in 1895 Frederic wrote the editor of the weekly *Black and White* that he had long been researching the O'Mahony family and their district in Munster. The stories are still works of fiction; however, the cathedral at Rosscarbery that figures in "The Truth of the Bishop," for instance, contrary to its fate in the story, was earlier, in 1582, taken over and turned into a Protestant property, but not demolished. While not intended to represent high historical scholarship, though, Frederic's stories do reflect his research on the O'Mahony settlements at Dunlougher, Ballydevlin, and Dunbeekin, near the moment of traditional Ireland's final destruction. Bridget Bennet, in her 1997 Frederic biography, describes his Irish historical research as "prodigious." The region in its flourishing Gaelic days is mentioned in O'Heerin's topographical poems:

> Ivehagha, most western part of Banba [Ireland],
> Is the great estate of O'Mahony
> A well-watered land of fair fortresses—
> Extensive are its brown nut producing plains.[46]

The extensive Irish historical scholarship undertaken throughout the nineteenth century would have provided Frederic with helpful material for the Ivehagh stories. Sir Thomas Stafford's *Pacata Hibernia: Ireland Appeased and Reduced: A History of the Wars in Ireland in the Reign of Queen Elizabeth*, for example, was

46. Quoted in "Topographical Appendix" to Geoffrey Keating's *The History of Ireland from the Earliest Period to the English Invasion*, trans. John O'Mahony (New York: Haverty, 1857), 701.

published in 1821. Richard Bagwell's *Ireland under the Tudors*, still a standard work, appeared in 1885. In 1892 the Cork Historical and Archeological Society began publication of its *Journal*. A variety of Irish historical materials came to be translated into English around this time as well. In 1892, three years before Frederic published his medieval tales, Standish O'Grady's translation of *Silva Gadelica: A Collection of Tales in Irish with Extracts Illustrating Persons and Places* was published. Other old Irish narratives were available as well: the O'Donovan translation of *The Annals of the Four Masters*, funded by the Royal Irish Academy, had appeared in 1854, and John O'Mahony's translation of Geoffrey Keating's seventeenth-century *History of Ireland* became available in 1857. In his novel *The Return of the O'Mahony*, Frederic also mentions, in addition to the *Four Masters*, other works such as the *Psalter of Rosbrin* and *The Annals of Innisfallen* (i.e., *Annals of Munster*). There would have been, or course, other influences, modern and historical, available as well—he was familiar as with Caesar Otway's *Sketches in Ireland* (1827), which included material relating to West Carbury—Skull, Dunmanus Bay, and Mount Gabriel.[47] In an 1893 essay, Frederic expressed his admiration for Emily Lawless's studies of the Irish West Coast life with which she was familiar.[48]

Turlogh O'Mahony, the chieftain of Dunbeekin, is not at all the formulaic hero of the popular medieval tale. When in "In the Shadow of Gabriel" he takes over leadership upon the death of his father, Fineen, in 1550, he is "a tall stripling of thin frame, with narrow shoulders and a pale, grave face." In this time before the foreign invasion, reading books and improving crop cultivation are more his inclination than battles. He has one foot in the ancient world and one in the dawning modern one. Lacking his father's strong, uncomplicated character, he is more thoughtful

47. Frederic mentions Otway's book in "The Coast of White Foam."
48. Frederic, "The Ireland of Today," 705.

and analytical than befits a chieftain of the feudal model, but he is not without resolve and is determined to fulfill the obligations that come with his leadership position. His men follow him as their duty, but they are not impressed with him. Given his sensitivity, his early efforts as chieftain are sometimes comical. He ventures to mount a party to investigate a light that is seen at night from an oak thicket on a shore within his domain. The story is that a terrible beast resides in those woods, running on all fours, and the smallest wave of his hand "will send the blood bursting from your ears." When Turlogh's coracle reaches shore, however, the five men he has with him on the expedition balk at going any farther. He tries to reason with them, even acknowledging that he knows they laugh at him behind his back, but his appeal is to no avail. Setting out on his own, he slips on a rock and falls in full view of his men, injuring his knee, but goes on. The investigation, to Turlogh's shock, proves to be something in the nature of a hero-venture, a dark journey into fear and trembling, and unfolds in a raging gothic storm. He finds that all his bearings and confidence—based on the spiritual assurances of a strange monk—are misguided and that the enemy is something quite other than a beast in the wood.

In "The Truce of the Bishop," set some fifty years later, after the turn of the century, Turlogh is now old and the English armies are ravaging the land. He and his people are hiding on the mountainside where they have fled and watched at night "the black forms of these English against the furnace they made of our corn and our roofs." Turlogh has proven over time to be a good leader and is now held in affection by his people—his wrinkled countenance has "sometimes the cunning of a fox, sometimes the wistful inquiry of a puzzled child; and they never feared him, and would always die for him, and understood when they heard men call him 'Turlogh of the Two Minds.'" He has not led his people into battles, however—neighboring bards mock his pacifism in their songs—and neither he nor his people are very skilled in warfare now that they are driven to the edge and "all things westward from Cork had been put to the sword." A ship appears offshore and turns out to be bearing the region's bishop, who has been on an extended pilgrimage abroad and is returning with a piece of the true cross to be placed on his high altar inland at his cathedral in Rosscarbery. Now mortally ill, he is a grotesque sight—"a swollen, black-swathed bulk, shapeless as a sack of corn ... bloated beyond human semblance," and knows nothing of what has befallen Ireland while he was in Europe. His young priest-servants, who fear and endlessly indulge him, are afraid to inform him of what has come to pass. Aware that he is finished, however, and that he will die here in Dunbeekin, he puts it upon Turlogh to see to the arrangements for a grand funeral replete with all imaginable ecclesiastical pageantry. Rosscarbery, a center of European learning in the medieval period, is now reduced to ruins, however, and occupied by Elizabethan troops. The Bishop's cathedral is rubble, and Turlogh's situation is uncanny—there are no cultural confirmations to guide his actions; his culture itself has been overwhelmed, and the story's conclusion is stark and shocking.

Turlogh is one of the characters in these stories who exemplify an essential human soundness that transcends his historical placement. He is not the one-dimensional warrior chieftain who can merely epitomize the violent tribal ethos as does the bewildered, "headstrong bullock" Murtogh in "The Path of Murtogh," a story as primitively brutal as an Icelandic revenge saga.[49] The Murtogh tale is far from simple, however, and reflects Frederic's sense of nuance and irony in its portrayal, for example, of Murtogh and Owny's funny-sad affection for each other and the powerful leader Murtogh's helpless erotic confusion sur-

49. The characterization "headstrong bullock" is that of Father Donatus, the priest in the story.

rounding his love for his young wife who secretly despises him. At the conclusion of "In the Shadow of Gabriel," having come into his own as chieftain through his trial in the oak wood, Turlogh chooses, by a benign lie, to go beyond the violent legacy he has received from his father and break the chain of murder and reprisal that otherwise would have ensued between the O'Mahonys and the O'Dwyers. In contrast, Murtogh's primitive mind is only delicately touched, troubled as it were, by oncoming events beyond his understanding. His father had heard read from a book at Rosbrin something that puzzles and intrigues Murty: "That the world turned around one way, like a duck on a spit, and the sun turned around the other way, and that was why they were apart all night. And often I come here, and I swear there is a movement under my feet." It is as if he eerily feels the impeding scientific century's approach, a century of ferment when, as Whitehead observed, "much was opened, new worlds, new ideas."[50] It is the atmosphere and mood that haunts the late sixteenth-century tales—no doubt reflecting their authorship in a period likewise in ferment.

Other characters of exemplary dignity occur throughout these tales. The dying bishop in "The Truce of the Bishop," Lawrence, son of Ivar, at first seems merely grotesque in his huge girth and relentless vanity, but he turns out in the end to be an exemplar of a courage and nobility that serve to galvanize the beaten Irish of Dunbeekin. His dying becomes the dying of all of them, and his "I abate no atom of my dignity" becomes, in effect, their epitaph, and this story, the concluding one in the present volume, captures the fall of the old Irish way of life, that historic cultural moment, perhaps as poignantly as has ever been done. Like Turlogh, Kate in "The Lady of Muirisc" transcends her backward social surroundings. The narrators of

50. Alfred North Whitehead, *Science and the Modern World* (New York: Mentor, 1960), 9.

"The Martyrdom of Maev," Brother Dunstan and Father Carew, and certainly Maev Carew herself, are also people of a simple nobility who navigate against the tempest roused when social-sexual taboos in country Ireland are violated. Hugh O'Sullivan in "The Wooing of Teige," as previously mentioned, represents a wise, grounded realism that contrasts with the fantasies of the O'Sullivan bard.

That the mild-mannered O'Sullivan lives in a poor retreat built into a cliff that is difficult to access, however, removed from the treacherous warfare going on in the world around him, problematizes the matter—such a retreat is necessary if he is to live the sane existence he chooses. Less fortunate is Turlogh—his enlightened bent serves him and his people well in terms of the living conditions he fosters and the peace that marks his rule, but finally, in "The Truce of the Bishop," the brutality reigning elsewhere has made its way along the coast, and now that the British armies have put Dunbeekin to the torch, he is compelled to adopt a single-minded, primitive focus. Though they go down with superb courage and grace, he and his people, having lost their war skills, are helpless before the onslaught; they represent to the invaders merely an unimportant part of mopping-up operations—raising again the question of whether a decent, liberalized life can be lived in a world of rampant savagery.

Another related concern evident in Frederic's writing is one on which Robert M. Myers has remarked. For all his focus on the cruelties of social backwardness and his positive representations of a new, modern consciousness dawning, as evident in Turlogh, Frederic shared with his Irish-American friend Louise Imogen Guiney, and many others at the time, a skepticism about modernity and its seeming association with physical and spiritual decline, a concern about the weakening effects of over-civilization.[51] Bishop Lawrence's tough, medieval courage con-

51. Myers, *Reluctant Expatriate*, 119.

trasts to the fumbling, uncertain behavior of the young priests around him. The foppish Spanish nobleman in the Murtogh tale suggests effeteness, and when Turlogh, no longer of two minds, turns perforce back to a primitive warrior's values, it would seem to further reflect Frederic's concern with how people can construct more liberal, humane cultures without being overwhelmed by unreconstructed others. Frederic would represent the same misgivings about modernity and civilized life, the sense of decline, in *Theron Ware* when, at the annual New York State Methodist convention the old ministers who had given their lives to the "wearing toil of itinerant missions through the rude frontier settlements" appear in starkly favorable contrast to the citified, newly ordained young men in whom "so plainly was it to be seen that they were not the men their forbears had been"[52]

Frederic's Irish stories are laced with such ironies and ambiguities as these and may reflect in that regard his decades, beginning in Utica, of trying to understand the Irish narrative he found so compelling and so contradictory. When he became disillusioned with the Irish political scene during his time, as Stanton Garner noted, it was in these Irish stories, "these delicate, handsome, and sensitive evocations of ... Ireland, that his love found expression."[53] His turning to the Irish West resulted in a distinctive literary achievement, an American writer's striking rendering of Ireland's tragic history as it unfolded in the secluded coastal bays and cliffs of the country's west, its wild Atlantic way.

52. Harold Frederic, *The Damnation of Theron Ware* (New York: Penguin, 1986), 2–3.
53. Garner, "Some Notes on Harold Frederic in Ireland," 74.

PART I

Chapter 1

THE MARTYRDOM
OF MAEV

I

Personally, I had nothing to do with the events which make this story. It was my fortune to meet and to know the chief actors in it before the drama began, in the days when they were smilingly unconscious of the parts that later they were to play and looked with clear-eyed, happy confidence upon their future. And when I came again upon the stage, the lights were out, the curtains drawn, and the players gone away. Yet what had happened between moved me so deeply then, and is still so succinctly and sharply graven in my memory, that it seems my story—at least to tell. It was in the early autumn of 1879 that I first visited the west of Ireland. We brothers of the Christian schools[1] do not travel much by way of pleasure, but it happened to me—no

Parts I and II of "The Martyrdom of Maev" appeared in *The New York Ledger*, Saturday, March 22, 1890. Parts III through VI appeared the following Saturday, March 29, 1890. The *Ledger*, a weekly published from 1855 through the 1890s, was the most famous and successful of the nineteenth-century American "storypapers." It paid its contributors well, having had at times a readership as high as 377,000.

1. This refers not to the Irish Christian Brothers but to a separate confraternity—the Brothers of the Christian Schools, or De La Salle Christian Brothers, founded in France by Saint Jean-Baptiste de la Salle around 1680.

matter how—that there was a fortnight to spare out of my year of schoolwork in England and that a vagrant whim led me to the remote, forlorn, and picturesquely tumbledown land of the O'Connors and O'Kellys. I am not a historian, much less am I an architect, yet some chance remarks that I had heard about the artistic value of the ancient abbey ruins at Balbarry, and the half-legendary associations of early saints and scholars and fierce sept[2] chieftains clustering around their dismantled walls, dictated my choice. To Balbarry I went—making my start in the early morning from that great desolation called Galway and reaching my goal in the gathering dusk of evening, after many wearisome miles of journeying by rail, by water, by coach, and lastly up a steep and rocky mountain road, in the rugless discomfort of an outside car.

Exhausting the experience might have been, but there was in it all a strange and powerful exhilaration of the senses. The rude and somber scenery; the cold sky piled with clouds, pushed gloweringly landward by Atlantic winds; the wide waste of barren mountain land and bog, with roofless towers, which medieval robbers had reared, standing guard over roofless cabins, whose owners had been turned into the ditch only last year; the unspeakable raggedness of the children we passed, and who raced madly after us for alms; the indescribable look of woe in the faces of the peasants; the squalor and gloom and hopelessness of it all—I grow sad now as I recall it, but my first impressions brought a sense of mental and spiritual expansion as well. It was like one's first reading of Dante.

The arrival at Balbarry[3] was in the nature of a disappointment. After driving for what seemed an hour, beside a high wall of masonry, inclosing what my driver called "The Hall," we turned an abrupt corner and came suddenly into the village—a

2. A clan or tribe.
3. Not actually a village in Connemara, the name at least is fictional.

wide and sprawling highway with whitewashed huts and plas-
tered houses leaning against one another in irregular groups
down both sides. Save for some lean pigs lounging idly in the
sterile gutter, some little children who looked wonderingly at
us from under their faded knit caps and shocks of unkempt
hair, and a brawny, well-fed constable with a rifle slung over his
shoulder,[4] who stopped to scowl inquiry at me, there were no
signs of life in the broad, bare street. I looked in vain for any evidence of that magnificent and inspiring past with which I had
come to commune. The present alone was visible, and it seemed
a very drear and dingy present.

To be the only guest in the solitary inn of the place—the
Barrymore Arms—did not minister to enlivenment. There appeared to be only two people employed at this hotel—a lame
and ragged old man who took my bag off the car and a gaunt,
sad-faced woman of middle age who showed me to my room—a
large and desolate chamber in the rear of the house. She lighted
a fire on the hearth and asked me plaintively would I be wanting
dinner, and would I be after having it served here in my room.
When I had assented to both propositions, she disappeared. I
had some moments of grim amusement a little later when, at-

4. Armed British police, members of the Royal Irish Constabulary, at least
a few of whom were posted in almost all towns throughout Ireland after 1822.
Members were often lured from the Irish population itself by the pay and sta-
tioned in areas to which they were not native. They provided a system whereby
Dublin Castle and London could maintain a constant surveillance of all points
in Ireland. Stephen Crane wrote in a piece titled "The Royal Irish Constabulary" in 1897: "One cannot look Ireland straight in the face without seeing a
great many constables. The country is dotted with little garrisons. It must have
been said a thousand times that there is an absolute military occupation. The
fact is too plain." He notes the way in which members of the constabulary were
demonstratively scorned by the people: "All through the South of Ireland one
sees the peasant turn his eyes pretentiously to the side of the road at the passing of the constable.... None looked, nodded, or gave sign. There was a line
drawn so sternly that it reared like a fence." *Crane Prose and Poetry* (New York:
Library of America, 1996), 978.

tracted by a prodigious squawking in the yard below my window, I looked out and beheld the lame old man chasing a hen about the enclosure, swooping at it with his battered hat and hobbling around in the pursuit like a grotesque brownie. He caught the fowl at last in a corner, and I turned away, with a sudden intuition that this was the first step in the preparation of my meal. There was not much appetite for the dinner when it came—particularly for the dish of fowl and bacon, which formed its staple feature—and my postprandial reflections, as I sat by the fire, were not of the highest sort. I feared me much that it had been a mistake—this visit to Balbarry.

But next morning, I was readily enough reassured. The sun was out, and his presence lent an aspect of cleanly cheeriness to the village high street. There were plenty of people about now, and their faces and manners and garb all interested me extremely. This was especially true of the women of the poorer sort, who, with their bare feet and ankles, their red petticoats and their long black cloaks with huge hoods drawn over their heads, were as quaint and unusual to the eye as if they had been Spanish or Servian.[5] The older of these were not always grateful to a closer inspection, for much living in cabins without chimneys gave their eyes a painfully inflamed appearance, and for the same reason, when I found myself crowded among them at the early mass in the little chapel, the odor of peat smoke from their garments was almost suffocating. But the air of novelty which everything and everybody wore was so charming that my mood for enjoyment was invincible, and when I called upon the priest and found that I knew some of his relatives in America— among them, one of my own order—it became doubly clear that I had made no mistake in coming to Balbarry.

At Father Carew's earnest invitation, I left the Barrymore Arms and took up my abode in the pastoral residence—a com-

5. Serbian.

modious old house on the main street, arranged in a fashion I had never seen before. The street door opened directly into a great kitchen floored with stone in places, with earth elsewhere, and roofed aloft with the upper beams and thatch of the house itself. There was a big chimney-place, and here the old female servant of his reverence sat all day long, bending over the peat embers which glowed on the hearth and crooning softly to herself, what time she was not preparing the meals. To one side of the chimney was a door leading into the pastor's part of the house, and the effect of the transition was notable; for here were carpets and books and modern furniture and lamps, and a grate for coal. The whole parish had free access to that outer room and came in and went as they liked, sitting on the benches in the chimney corner and smoking a pipe with old Maggie, or even wheedling her into giving them food and drink on occasion. But there were only a few—substantial people with education and ideas in their heads—who ever saw the inside of Father Carew's own abode.

The priest was not alone an amiable host; he was the central figure of the village, knew everybody, and dominated everything roundabout. He had greater knowledge, greater authority, greater confidence, and, it ought to be added, greater and more uniform good spirits than anyone else. If much that was going on in the countryside grieved his heart and tempted his soul to rebellion against the cruelly tragic farce of misrule and mischance which blighted his country, you caught no sign of it on his smooth brow or in his equable glance. There were no Protestants in this part, unless, indeed, some of the alien constabulary—who inhabited the best house in the village, lower down the street—might belong under that head. But I fancied that Father Carew would be just the man to get on well with them all, if they had half-filled his village.

He was not a deeply read man, but he knew a good deal

about the history of this wild region and had a considerable interest in the ruins which I had come to explore. They took on a
new value in my eyes when he pointed them out to me; it was
like being shown over a battlefield by a general.

There was an abbey which was believed to be of St. Patrick's
foundation, and there was a castle which, no doubt, one of the
first De Burghs[6] had built, and both were close together, and in
that sweepingly disheveled state that only Irish ruins attain. To
get to these, you turned off the main street, and wandered down
through a tangle of narrow, foul alleys (where I came to learn
that most of the population and all of the pigs of Balbarry lived),
and crossed the marketplace of the old town, and past under an
ancient gateway through a deserted churchyard overgrown with
nettles and littered with broken tablets and sunken tombstones,
and emerged into a new maze of alleys even muddier and more
squalid than the others. The ruins were here—all about and
above and below you, in bewildering plenitude and confusion.
I never made quite sure where the abbey left off and the castle
began, and it was always a fine uncertainty as to what had been
erected by the monks and the routers of the dark ages and what
by the very modern gombeen man,[7] a corn factor who had ac-
quired possessions in this quadrant of the town. But it was all
highly curious and novel, and the magnificent margin left for
speculation and theory only added to the content with which I
moused and mused about the ruins. I found a great many in-

6. The De Burghs were Norman settlers in thirteenth-century Galway.
7. "Gombeen man" refers to a despised Irish type—the local, philistine
merchant who held himself above and apart from the ordinary rural people and
often loaned rent money to the desperate at high interest. The Irish poet Joseph
Campbell described a store-keeper of this sort in his poem "The Gombeen": "Behind a web of bottles, bales, / Tobacco, sugar, coffin nails / The gombeen like a
spider sits, / Surfeited; and, for all his wits, / As meager as the tally-board / On
which his usuries are scored...." *The Poems of Joseph Campbell*, ed. Austin Clarke
(Dublin: Figgis, 1963), 117.

teresting and suggestive things. I made some drawings of rare Gaelic decorations and devices, and I secured for my mind a helpful season of rest and change.

Even more famous, locally, than the ruins, I discovered, was a cavern a mile or so from the village, at the bottom of which coursed a shallow subterranean river, and I went with Father Carew one day to view this phenomenon. There had been an abbey here, too, and ample ruins remained, but they had small archaeological interest, having existed only a mere six hundred years, which is the yesterday of Irish history. At the bottom of what seemed to have been the orchard, there was a heap of great stones, irregularly piled. A witch-like old woman had come after us when we turned through the fields toward the ruins, and she joined us now, with a large wisp of straw in her hand. She clambered over the boulders, and we followed her. She disappeared from sight, and we, coming to the place, saw her far below us, gliding with a curious, jerking motion down a flight of damp stone stairs, spaciously set into the earth. We followed her down—there must've been sixty or more of these steps—groping our way in the growing darkness, till at last we felt, rather than saw, that the bottom had been reached. Then the hag, who had awaited our coming, set fire to her straw and held it high aloft with one skinny arm, pointing before her with the other. By the red light we saw a black, oily surface of water under the immense overhanging rock in front—water which seemed to slide rather than flow, so sinuous was the effect of its slow progress. That was all. The straw was burned out, and we made our way up once more to daylight and fresh air.

Father Carew spoke some words in the Erse[8] to the old crone as he gave her a coin, but she went mumbling off with a pretense of not understanding his question. When I asked him what

8. The Irish language. The term "Erse" is rarely used anymore.

he had said, he replied: "Oh, many's the time I've asked her the same—where are the other caverns? But they'll never tell me—though my word for it, scores of 'em know."

From his further explanations, I learned that this hidden river was known to have other cavernous approaches in the vicinity, but that the secret of their location was closely guarded by those who had it. These caves had, according to popular tradition, been hiding places for refugees as far back as the Whiteboy days.[9] From that time to this, the occult knowledge had been handed down from one political secret society to another. Countless generations of the Dalys and Farleys living in the wild glens of the neighborhood had kept the secret alive. They were parishioners of his, no doubt, but that did not help Father Carew to get to the mystery of the caves.

"The omadhauns!"[10] he concluded, with a shade of pique on his face. "As if they couldn't trust me!" But not all my time was spent among ruins and rocks. There was pleasant human society in Balbarry, to which Father Carew unlocked the door for me. My story, however, has to do with only one of the families I met in the ancient village during my fortnight's stay.

I shall not forget the impression produced upon me by Mrs. Carew, the widow of a second cousin of my host, when I first saw her in the small, shadowy parlor of her own house. She was tall, erect, and slender of figure, with a pale, gentle face, a soft, clear voice, and eyes that had in them both wisdom and a sense of sadness. The courtesy with which she welcomed us could not have been of finer fiber in a princess. There was so little light in the room that I gained no notion of her real age but supposed her

9. The Whiteboys were a clandestine late eighteenth-century Irish organization devoted to fostering and carrying out agrarian rebellion against landlords and their agents. Wearing white smocks, the group raided at night, burning barns and generally destroying the property of the landlord class as best they could.

10. Irish, meaning fools, idiots.

to be not older than myself, until, when we had taken our seats, she spoke of her married children away in the United States. Then, looking more closely, I saw that at least sixty years must have passed over her head—though they had scarcely silvered its brown bands of hair, combed simply from a central parting across the temples, and had failed altogether in aging either voice or glance. She had been born a Martin, a very good family, and Tyrone; her husband had now been dead nearly twenty years; and of all her children (there were two married sons in one of the Pacific states, a married daughter in Minnesota, and another daughter in a convent), only the youngest remained at home with her—the maiden Maev.

I remember that the sweetness and fitness of this beautiful old Gaelic name were apparent to me even before I saw the damsel who bore it. The daughter of such a woman—so gracious a realization in herself of what was uniquely delicate and fine in Irish womanhood—ought to have, I felt, a name like that, with its fragrance of an ancient poetry and faith.

Maev Carew entered the room anon, and, at her mother's bidding, busied herself in preparing for us some small refreshment. She was very like what I fancied the elder lady must have been at her age—tall and graceful and fair-faced as a star. She served us silently, with the shyness of smile and bow which for the instant almost oppressed me with a sense of artificiality. But soon enough, I saw that it was wholly genuine, and that I had mistaken it because it was a survival from a civilization strange to me. The girl was convent-bred, but there was something more needed to account for the courtly diffidence, if I may use the phrase, of her demeanor toward Father Carew and myself. From being surprised at it, I grew to watching it with an approving eye, and then to saying to myself that I had never seen anything to compare with it for charm of modesty and deference and earnestness of welcome combined. Thus a princess of Thomond[11] might have borne herself in her father's hall, greeting the guests of the sept. Her manner was as Gaelic as her name. And she was very beautiful as well.

The girl joined but rarely in the hour conversation which followed, speaking only when directly addressed. Then her answers were the index to a bright, well-nurtured mind and a good heart. She seemed to have devolved upon her, or to have assumed from choice, a general supervision of charitable work in the broad and needy parish. Father Carew's questions related almost entirely to this, I noticed, and she seemed to have special knowledge on the subject. I knew that the poverty of this region was very grievous, and that it was in the power of the priest to do painfully little for its relief. But I thought that even this little must have an air of coming from heaven itself when administered by Maev's hand.

Just as twilight was gathering, and we were about to leave, a young man came in, and the priest introduced him to me as his friend, Mitchel Daunt. It was a fine, clear, open face that this newcomer had, crowned with curling, fair hair and lighted by frank eyes. I liked him on the instant, as we shook hands, and then, at the priest's sign, sat down again.

Mitchel was as characteristic, in his way, as I had found Maev to be—though, perhaps, the type he represented was more modern than hers. His countenance was of that curious classical regularity which some Irish priests, most Irish patriots, and all Irish actors exhibit—the chiseled features and thin, arched lips, having inward curves at their corners. I fancy that this face, which we continually find reproduced in America, even among young men whose grandparents left Ireland, is due not so much to race as to the traditions of monkish, clean-shaven visages that have for centuries been so familiar in the Island of Saints. It is a face

11. Irish Kingdom in north Munster in the tenth and eleventh centuries.

which goes with the fervid temperament, a strong personality, a ready mind, and deep capacity for likes and dislikes.

I learned that young Mitchel was to marry Maev when he had made a home for her. His father was a tenant farmer living some miles west of Balbarry—a man of more-than-common refinement, who had formerly been well-to-do but now was much reduced through the decay of agriculture and the poorness of his land. The son had been educated at Tuam[12] and had learned civil engineering, at which he was now working in Balbarry, but his chances for success here were discouraging, and so he was going to America—to Baltimore—where an opening was offered him. Indeed, barely a month remained for him in Ireland before he was to sail from Queenstown.

I took a great interest in these young people during the rest of my stay in Balbarry. They seemed devoted to each other, which was in itself an argument for liking. And then they were so splendidly confident of their future—of Mitchel's success in the states, of the fine home they should have out there, and of the delight that was to come through also having with them, after a little, both Mitchel's parents and old Mrs. Carew. A wonderful glow would come into Maev's great gray eyes, with their dark sweeping lashes and depths of mingled smiles and sober reverie, as she listened to our talks about all this. Oh yes! Nothing could be more certain than that Mitchel would succeed and would come back for her.

I gave the young man some letters to friends of mine in Baltimore who might be of service to him. And when I had finally said goodbye to them all, and had started down the mountainside on my journey back to England and to work, the truth is that I thought a good deal about these honest people of Balbarry, and mighty little about its medieval ruins.

12. Town some twenty miles north of Galway city.

II

Nearly five years went by before I saw Ireland again. Most of this interval had been spent in France, which means that very little news from the outside world reached me. From time to time I did, in truth, hear vague reports of the famine in Ireland, of the rise of the Land League, of the Coercion laws, of cruel evictions in the West, of the imprisonment of popular leaders and even of patriotic women, and of the general melancholy and turbulent condition of the country.[13] But there were few details in the Paris journals, and perhaps I did not follow very closely even such accounts as were printed. At all events, it never occurred to me to connect Balbarry and its simple, goodhearted, out-of-the-way folk with the national disorders and troubles.

In the summer of 1884, my health suddenly gave way. I had worked too hard and needed rest and change in a cooler climate than that of the Loire Valley. I had often told the scholarly superior of our little Angevin[14] community, Brother Mémoire, about the wealth of odd ecclesiastical remains in Ireland, and it was he who suggested that we should go there together—I to recover strength and serenity of nerves and he to accumulate archaeological facts which might help him with his learned book on "The Conversion of Brittany." Thus the trip was arranged.

We did not this time go direct to Balbarry, but, after some days spent at various historic sites, approached it by another

13. The "lesser famine" of 1879, *An Gorta Beag*, was in fact very grievous in Connacht where this story occurs. The years referred to here, roughly 1879 to 1884, were characterized by increased political agitation spurred by the crop failures and food shortages along with rising rents. The Land League, seeking to coordinate Irish protest movements against these conditions, was founded in Mayo in 1879. The harsh "coercion laws" represented British attempts to suppress rebellious political organizations in Ireland. The Protection of Persons and Property Act of 1881, for example, allowed for imprisonment of persons without trial.

14. Relating to the Anjou region in the Loire Valley.

route, involving a long day's journey on the top of a coach, over a wild and mountainous road. Here, as everywhere else in the country, the story of the past five years was told by the increased number of roofless cabins and of constables with rifles slung over their shoulders. These two things are in the gloomy foreground of every picture of Ireland which my memory calls up.

We were to stop at a certain town on the road for dinner—a midday meal for which the sharp air of the hills had given us famous appetites. Ordinarily, this stop was for an hour, but some accident to the running gear of the huge vehicle rendered our stay this day a matter of at least two hours. We had time to see something of the place, and, as a wise preliminary to this, we called upon the parish priest. He had both affability and leisure, and acted as our guide. He neither knew nor cared much about the antiquities of the town, but his whole heart was wrapped up in the local convent, and to this we were straightway led. It would have been unseemly for us to grumble, for the good pastor would have been greatly surprised to find that religious institutions were not our chief and abiding desire, and besides, there was a legend that St. Conchenna had founded the nunnery and this mollified Brother Mémoir.[15]

The buildings themselves were of considerable size and depressingly new. The priest presented us to the mother superior, and we were shown about the public portions of the place. We visited the schoolroom and heard the pupils sing some exhibition songs in our honor—very badly, Brother Mémoir said, after we had got out. We saw the recreation ground, the chapel, the workrooms, the kitchens—all in wearisome detail. Finally, as a climax, we were led to the pride of the convent, the display of laces made by the nuns and their pupils. These fabrics, no doubt very remarkable and beautiful, were shown in glass

15. St. Conchenna of Killevey in Armagh. She died, according to the *Annals of the Four Masters*, in 654 AD.

cases, and our guide in this apartment was a tall young nun, whose veil deeply surrounded her face. My French companion displayed great interest in the laces and bent eagerly over the frames. I, after a polite, cursory glance, stood talking with the priest and casually mentioned that we were going to Balbarry. He offered to give me a letter to a linen draper there, whom he knew. I thanked him but explained that I had friends there— among them Father Carew and his relative, Mrs. Carew, and her daughter, who, by this time, must be married and settled in life. As I mentioned these names, the nun gave a sudden start and involuntarily turned toward me, bending an intense and piercing scrutiny upon my face from beneath the shadow of her veil.

The action and the gaze were so unexpected—so little to be looked for within this house of silent, shadowy figures and downcast eyes—that I stared back at her in mute surprise. It was only after she had turned again, and moved toward the door, that I began to be conscious of a recollection of having seen that face, those eyes, before. For a moment it baffled me. For one thing, the countenance, with white bands at brow and chin, and in the shrouding gloom of the great veil, was only elusively like some other I remembered, and there was in the look that had peered forth so strangely at me a wild, almost terrified expression, which I had never seen in mortal eyes before, yet they were familiar—strikingly, insistently familiar. All at once, in a flash, it dawned upon me. The nun was Maev Carew!

I could not be mistaken. These were the selfsame eyes that I had seen in the little parlor at Balbarry. Alas! Then they had suggested only the sweet trustfulness and candor of happy maidenhood. And now—what mournful mystery was in the glance they gave me, as from the somber recesses of a shroud?

The discovery that the suffering nun was Maev Carew so startled and shocked me that I made my way abruptly out of the lace room and down the long corridor toward the main en-

trance. The priest and Brother Mémoir followed on, and over-
took me at the door.

"Tell me," I said hurriedly to the priest when we stood in the
open air once more. "Am I right?—I used to know her family
well—was not the sister we just saw formerly a Miss Carew—of
Balbarry?"

"That was her name before she became a religious," said the
pastor, with a new note of formality in his tone. Evidently, he
was vexed at my uncivil want of interest in the convent, which
he quite pardonably regarded with pride as an ornament to his
parish.

"In the name of all the saints, what has happened to her?
She looked at me as if she saw a ghost."

"There was some trouble," he answered, even more stiffly. "I
do not rightly know the story. Ye may hear it at Balbarry, if ye
are so very well known there."

So he was annoyed, too, with my having declined the letter
to his friend, the draper. We thanked him for his courtesy and
made our farewells, hurrying back to our coach.

Brother Mémoir, I fear, found me slow company for the re-
mainder of the journey. I answered his questions and remarks
in the vaguest and most slipshod manner. My mind fastened itself resolutely upon that weird glance from under the nun's veil
and turned over a thousand hypotheses by which to account
for it and for Maev's presence there. Grave trouble of some sort
there must have been. Its nature I could not guess. But some
terrible calamity must have burst upon the peaceful little fold I
knew of and broken its shelter down and scattered its inmates.
I could think of nothing but this, and I almost trembled as we
neared Balbarry, with fear of what I should learn.

The village street down which I passed once more gave few
evidences of change. There were more constables visible, and,
apparently, fewer pigs. But nothing else seemed altered. The

same limping old man came out from the yard of the Barry-more Arms for our luggage, and the same gaunt female showed us to our rooms. Both recognized me but neither displayed the slightest interest in the fact of my return. I had an uncomfortable sense of the uncanny in the chilling, matter-of-course manner of their reception—as if they had known all along that I must come back and had impassively waited for me, as time with his scythe and hourglass waits for all men.

I learned from the woman that Father Carew was still the parish priest and that the Widow Carew still lived in the house she had always occupied. When I asked, with a stumbling tongue, if her daughter Maev was still with her, the woman looked me over and answered coldly: "She is not"—and turned away.

The fact that the Irish peasantry almost never say "yes" or "no" but couch their replies in that indirect form which the Erse tongue employs was not new to me. Yet the roundabout negative of the landlady, or chambermaid, or whatever she was seemed to have a sour and forbidding emphasis which plain "no" could never have worn.

I could not resist the temptation to go out before dinner and strive to get some light upon the dark problem which troubled me. My companion was glad enough to be left behind to rest and read his guidebooks. I went down the main street, my steps instinctively leading me toward the priest's house.

As I drew near the pastoral residence, a tall woman, deeply hooded in the custom of the district, emerged from it and came slowly down the path toward me. She walked haltingly, and as one in feeble health, and I assumed her to be some invalid parishioner who had been in to pass an hour by the chimney corner with old Maggie. It was not until she had almost passed me that I recognized in her Mrs. Carew.

I lifted my hat on the instant and stopped to speak with her, stretching out my hand. She looked wonderingly at me, making a half-bow in response to my salutation, but evidently not in the least recalling me to mind. In the single glance, I saw that she had aged sadly. Her form was no longer erect: the gentle face was wan and marked with lines of melancholy, and the eyes searched my face with the dim wistfulness of failing sight.

"I am Brother Dunstan, Mrs. Carew," I said. "Do you not remember me—here—five years ago?"

"Oh, entirely!" she answered, after a moment's pause, and gave me her hand in a hesitating way. "And are you very well?" she asked. I could see that she only partially recognized me, even now, and was vainly striving to fit my image into its proper associations in her memory.

"You gave Mitchel the letters!" she said at last, suddenly, and with something like the old light in her face. She took my hand again. "Oh, well, indeed I remember you."

The light passed from her countenance as swiftly as it had dawned. Her head drooped again, and she drew the great, black cloak more closely about her throat. Then she said, with infinite pathos: "My heart took grief when the poor lamb—went from me." The voice quavered and broke as she turned her face away. So, with bowed head, the old lady passed up the street. I forbore to offer her my company to her door. Her grief was sacred against intrusion.

Father Carew remembered me upon the instant and gave me a hearty and even strenuous welcome. He had so portentous a quarrel ready over my having gone again to the inn and insisted so firmly on proceeding at once with me to fetch Brother Mémoir that there was no gainsaying him. We both became guests at the pastorate within the hour.

After dinner, as we sat in the good priest's library—the evening air in these high latitudes was cool enough, I remember, for a fire on the hearth—I asked him, all at once:

"Tell me what happened to young Mitchel and sweet Maev?

I have seen poor Mrs. Carew, and I know the story must be a sad and cruel one."

"Faith—you're right!" said the priest.

And this is the story as he told it to me. I cannot reproduce his soft Connaught accent, nor would I if I could; for the rest, the language is as nearly his own as may be.[16]

III

You were here in September, was it not, of 1879? Well, you would have heard speak, even then, of the failure of the potatoes. You might not have noticed it; it would have had small meaning for you. But for my people up here, it meant life and death.

There had been no good harvest since '76, and rents everywhere were more or less in arrears. To have the smallest potato crop in twenty years come atop of this was terrible, but it was not the worst. We are used to tightening our belts for want of a meal of victuals. Short rations we could have borne; perhaps there's no people on God's footstool give so little thought to eating as the Irish. But the landlords—they've no notion of abating their tax on us by a ha'penny, in bad times or good. And the rents had to be paid.

The land here doesn't produce rents. In the best of seasons, it's all the tenant can do to get a living out of it. His rent he must find somewhere else. This he does in many ways: he gets odd day's work, here and there, in the neighborhood; he gets, maybe, some help from relations in America; he borrows as much as he can from the gombeen man, at ruinous rates of interest; and in the fall he goes to England to help in the harvesting and brings back a few pounds.

Well, this year, God help us, all these things failed. Times were bad in England, and they had idle laborers of their own to

16. The narrator thus shifts in part III. Father Thomas Carew narrates parts III through V and Brother Dunstan resumes as narrator in part VI.

spare. Times were bad in America, and next to no money came from there.[17] So everything was lost. Do you follow me? We are gamblers up here—compelled by law to bet on a game that the landlords control. The small tenant, poor devil, wagers that the harvest will be fine and that he will earn enough money outside to pay his rent. If he wins, all he wins is the privilege of continuing to live. If he loses, he is kicked out into the ditch.

In this bad '79, my poor people lost all around. They had taken no money and wages; they had much less food than they needed to see them through the winter. This meant both hunger and eviction—a nightmare for us all.

As the days began to shorten, stories were whispered of troubles in other parts. Something they called the Land League was started in Dublin. Meetings were being held to demand reductions, and the government sent more police into the West and refused to listen. The winter looked black enough ahead of us. So near as I could make out, my parish owed seventeen hundred pounds arrears in rent, and there were not seventeen hundred farthings among us. The agent of our landlord, Mr. Keene, a heavy, square-jawed, sour squireen from the other side of the lake, was known to be a hard man, and we looked to him for no mercy. As for the landlord himself, we hadn't seen him since he was a boy, and no one expected to see him again. It had been twenty years since an Earl of Concannon was last at Balbarry Hall.

Yet, lo and behold this landlord did come to us, just in what seemed the nick of time. And before he had been at the Hall a week, we were all blessing our fortune in having so good-hearted and fine a man to deal with instead of Mr. Keene.

Lord Concannon arrived quite unexpectedly at the Hall, and the day after his coming he sent for me to lunch with him. He was a decent young fellow, three or four and twenty, tall and

17. The depression of the 1880s and 1890s in the United States was severe— the worst in American history prior to that of the 1930s.

good-looking, and very simply dressed. His talk was that of a well-read man, and indeed he was only then fresh from an English university. He told me that what he had heard and read of the distress in Connaught had made him ashamed of neglecting his duties and that he had come to be with his people and see for himself their condition and needs.

Sure, I could have fallen on his neck when I heard this. The Considines had been lords hereabouts for centuries, and all ruffians and robbers, so far as the best of us could learn. But here was one, faith, who was honest and kindly, and not only wanted to do good but was willing to be rightly guided in the doing of it. It was this last that was so novel, and that made him in my eyes a white crow among Irish landlords.

When I had told him of my delight at his words, and we talked a while, he said to me: "Father Carew, your name sets me to thinking. Haven't I some relations here of that same name? I remember some boys here, years ago, whose mother was a Martin of Tyrone, like my grandmother. The two would be cousins, or something of the sort. The father of these boys was the village doctor, and a gentleman."

"He's long since dead," I answered. "He was my cousin. The boys you remember are out in Oregon these six years, but their mother lives here still, and there's no finer lady in all of Ireland."

"I'll walk down with you," said the young man, "and call on her. There are not so many of my kin left that we can afford to be strangers." At this he took his hat and stick, and strolled with me along the high street and to the widow's house.

I thought it was a fine thing of him, and I still think that he meant this, and all else he did, well. Mrs. Carew was at home, and later on Maev came in. They were surprised at his visit, and not altogether easy in their minds about its purport, but they wouldn't have been themselves if they hadn't been polite and courteous to him. He said to them much that I have already described—about his sense of responsibility as a landlord and his desire to do good among his people. They could not but be delighted with this, and the young man himself was of the likable sort, an easy and pleasant talker, and modest with it all.

It was so plain that he had enjoyed his visit, and had made a good impression as well, that when we got outside I took occasion to tell him that Maev was betrothed to young Mitchel Daunt, a son of one of his tenants, who had only just gone to America to prepare a home for her.

His lordship didn't seem very enthusiastic over this information.

"A tenant's son?" he asked. "Surely that is beneath her."

"Young Daunt is a civil engineer," I replied, and "a graduate of Tuam—a fine, manly, promising lad. You must remember," I added, "that though they are well related, these ladies are poor and think no harm of belonging to the people. They do not hold themselves above Mitchel Daunt."

"Why, for that matter, we all belong to the people," he answered with a smile. And so our talk ended.

Well, a month went on like this, until we were close upon Christmas. We heard worse and worse stories of distress and discontent roundabout. God forgive us! Perhaps we bore our neighbors' grief with too light a heart that our own good luck so turned our heads. Lord Concannon asked for nothing better than to be shown what to do. I myself took over the small holdings scattered in the bog and up on the mountainside. He was all compassion and shame for what he saw, and called himself a beast for having ever taken ha'penny from the poor devils planted up there, where all that isn't stone is bad black swamp. He swore he'd wipe off all their arrears with a sponge on his slate. His mind was full of plans for starting works which would give these creatures employment, and meantime he gave me fifty pounds for my poor.

One fine evening—'twas a couple of nights before Christmas—the young lord came down here to take a bite and sup with me, and talk over his grand scheme for the tenants, and I had something on my tongue to tell him, too, if so be it a good chance came. For I had heard some stray words spoken by one of the glen women that troubled me. They're a wild lot, the Farleys and Dalys, out by the underground river—you went there with me, you remember—and they mistrusted the landlord, no matter what good he did, and some spiteful tongue among them had let slip the hint that Lord Concannon was behaving in this fine way because Maev Carew had bewitched him with her smiles. Now, the very breath of such talk as this is poison to a girl's good name in these parts, and so I had it in mind to advise his lordship to go less to the widow Carew's house. Not that there was an evil thought in his head, or that Maev had ever a notion of anyone else but Mitchel across the sea, but there must be no whisper of such a thing for uncharitable people to roll over in their mouths.

Well, we sat here in this very room, smoking after our meal, and I busy thinking how I should say these things to him without offense, when there came a big rap on the door.

"Come in," called I.

Faith, who should open the door there and stick in his ugly, bull-necked head but Mr. Keene, the agent! The moment I caught sight of his scowling, hang-jowled face, I felt in my bones that there was mischief afoot.

He never gave so much as a glance at me but looked straight at my guest, and there was a wicked devil grinning out of his eyes as he did so.

"Why, my Lord," said the agent, after glaring maliciously at my guest, "your uncle the Honorable Michael Considine has arrived from Dublin tonight, and he's at the hall awaiting you. That was his message."

Mr. Keene cocked his evil eye triumphantly at me when he had said this.

"Wait for me outside," said the earl after a moment's dumbfounded silence, and the agent took the hint and disappeared.

His lordship stood up, and I helped him with his topcoat. He muttered something about the necessity of hastening to greet his uncle, but it wasn't welcome that was written on his face. He shook hands with me on parting with a confused manner I'd never seen in him before.

"I may send for you to come up to my place tomorrow," he said, as he went out into the night.

Well, I never laid eyes on Lord Concannon from that day to this. He left Balbarry the next day, with no farewell word, good, bad, or indifferent, to any soul in the parish, and he's not stepped foot in Ireland since.

I waited indoors that day for the summons to go up to the Hall, which never came, and in some way I failed to learn about the young man's departure. In fact, few people knew it that day, for he went off as quietly as he could.

But next morning—the blessed Christmas Day—the air was black with rumors. There was a mass before daybreak, and even then sinister stories were afloat. By night, what with the gossip of the servants of the Hall and the reports brought to me, I knew pretty well what had happened. The Honorable Michael, a hard, clever, greedy man, had been warned by the agent that his nephew was destroying the Balbarry property. He had posted straight to Ireland and to Balbarry at this news. It was a stormy four hours of it they two had that night together, but it could have only one ending. The earl was a weak, young man, and the Honorable Michael was a strong, old man. The arguments the uncle used I can only guess at. Whatever they were, they won the fight. And Lord Concannon, having yielded against his will, was ashamed to look me or his tenants in the face again and sneaked away like a coward—he that I had looked to for such brave, fine conduct.

When the coach came in that Christmas evening, there were eight constables on top, all with their guns and cow-skin haversacks. The Honorable Michael had telegraphed for them. Wirra! Wirra! The sun seemed never to shine on Balbarry after that.

Within a day or two, bailiffs came down from Dublin with a bushel of writs for eviction. The whole week was spent serving them on the luckless tenants in arrears—which meant four-fifths of my parish. The poor devils were frightened out of their five senses. Some rushed to the gombeen man to pledge everything short of their souls for a little ready money. Some went to the Hall and groveled before Mr. Keene, and gave up their leases in exchange for others at much higher terms. And some of those who had enough money to pay their rents, I'm ashamed to say, began to plan to take over the holdings from which the others were to be evicted. For the League was young yet, and land-grabbing hadn't been put under the ban by the tenants all standing together. It was a scrabble of selfishness then, and the foul fiend took the hindmost.

I'll not weary you with the heartaching story of the next few months. More police were drafted in, and then some soldiers as well. A hundred and twelve families were evicted—the roofs of their cabins torn off, and the human beings put out into the winter with no shelter and no food. Faith, I remember little about it all myself, for I went nearly crazy with rage and vexation and overwork.

Once I went to the Hall and forced Michael Considine himself to see me. But it was small good to me or my people. What I said made no mark on him—the cold, mean, old creature—and when I had finished, he turned on me and warned me that priests could go to prison as well as laymen, and that if I hadn't a care he would lay me by the heels in Galway jail as a "barrater"—whatever that means[18]—under a law of Edward the Third. So I went away not terrified at all but sick at heart with the hopelessness of it all. And the worst of the evictions came after that.

The event of them all was when old Patrick Daunt and his wife were put out from the farm they had ruined themselves in trying to keep up. Mitchel's father was a man of standing in the community, a fine old character whom everybody liked and respected. It was known that he was heavily in arrears, but it had not been dreamed that he could be treated like the poor cotters on the hillside. Yet out he went, and his farm was handed over to a land-grabber from across the Lake, a friend of Keene's named Mangan. The shock turned poor Daunt's mind. He got a big boat from a neighbor and put it upside down on the roadside, in front of his old house, and began living in it with his wife. She, poor woman, was far from strong, but she stuck by her husband. There, in the roadside, they lived huddled in their boat or crouched over a miserable fire outside in the ditch, watching their old home and cursing the Mangans whenever they showed their heads. Pitying neighbors brought them food but vainly offered them shelter as well. Time and time again, I went to them and strove by entreaty and by sharp scolding to get them away and to my house. Poor Maev went often, both with me and by herself, to beg the old couple to come to the village and make a home with her and her mother. But Daunt, in his growing madness, would exchange no words with the girl, and at last, one day, cursed her as a friend to Lord Concannon, who had brought all this misery on the countryside.

The girl came to me in her grief, weeping as if her heart would break at this injustice and her helplessness. And when I strove to comfort her, she told me that others had thrown this same reproach in her face. I promised her that next day I

18. "Barratry" in law generally refers to persons illegally stirring up violence and discord in order to profit from it themselves.

would go again to the Daunts and force them out of their folly if needs be.

I went next day, and on the roadside, beside the boat, there was a group of excited peasants. In the center of this cluster of sympathetic neighbors was a white-haired, growling, bent old man I scarcely recognized. It was Patrick Daunt, and he was stark mad!

"Glory be to God! You've come, Father," some one of the bystanders called out to me; "we were after starting to fetch you."

Something in the tone of this voice frightened me, and as I looked at the speaker, there rose close beside me the shrill wail of an old keener. I turned and glanced at the boat, which I saw now had been turned right-side up. The crowd made way for me to see.

In the boat lay poor old Mrs. Daunt, quite dead.

IV

Well, this double tragedy made Balbarry very famous. A young professional man of the neighborhood, who is now, to my mind, our best talker in Parliament, came here and learned the facts, and made a speech about them, which set Ireland afire. The government sent him to prison for it, but he had done his work.[19] Journalists came to see the boat the poor Daunts had lived in

19. The reference here to the young man who is now "our best talker in Parliament" is to Frederic's friend Timothy Healy and, as mentioned in the preface, a reference to an actual event as well. Near Bantry in 1878, a man named Michael McGrath, evicted from his home, sheltered himself and his family under an inverted boat. Healy and some other Land Leaguers confronted the "land-grabber" who took over the property from which the McGraths had been evicted, and Healy was prosecuted and jailed for being a party to the intimidation of the new owner. Years later, Healy recalled the McGrath case in a speech in parliament: "He remembered the state in which the husband was buried, the corpse taken out of the boat, the rain pouring down as the priest said the last absolution, and McGrath was a decent, substantial tenant before his cruel eviction." Callanan, *T. M. Healy*, 45.

and to report their sad story. It was printed in London; it was cabled to America in full. And everywhere it made a great stir.

It was a double funeral they had, too, for Patrick Daunt died of a stroke, even while they were taking him next day to the madhouse. And this part of the country had never before seen, and is not likely, God forbid, to ever see again, such an outpouring of mourners. Faith, I had no notion that there were so many people in all Connemara as came here to follow our martyrs to their grave. The men brought their sticks with them, and when the procession passed the gates of the Hall up yonder, the air was thick with curses and the old women's cries for vengeance. The Honorable Michael Considine, I can tell you, kept well in his hole after *that*, and Keene, the agent, took two constables with him for safety wherever he went.

Poor Maev wrote the sad details of the tragedy to Mitchel. It rested heavy on her soul that, the last time she saw his father, the old man cursed her, and she came to see me in her trouble to ask if in honor she was bound to put that in her letter. I told her "no," of course. She showed me the letter before she sent it, and, faith, no tenderer or sweeter words were ever put to so mournful a tale. It was like *her*—that's the best description you can have of it.

Strange enough, there came no reply to this letter. Mitchel had written to her very regularly before that, but now three months went by and still no answer from him. Then we feared he must be ill, and I wrote to my friends in Baltimore, begging them to give us word of the young man.

Meanwhile, there came upon us something as terrible in its way as the ruthless evictions. It was not, like those, an open and public calamity. We could neither see nor feel it. It made no noise. When we talked of it, our words were in whispers. Nobody knew about it, but nobody thought of anything else. Have you guessed what this secret and sinister something was? Our name for it here is moonlighting.

One morning—this would have been in February—a farmer coming down the lake road with a load of turf found Mr. Keene's pony loose on the roadside, or it would have been loose save that the car was wedged in the ditch, where the beast had dragged it off the highway. There was blood on the seat of the driver and on the steps of the car. It was a lonely bog over which the road ran here, with clumps of furze scattered along the road, on the fringe of the black waste. From behind one of these, the farmer heard groans, and he left his donkey to see what was to pay.

Mr. Keene lay there, where he had dragged himself for shelter through the night. He had been shot down off his car the evening before, as he was driving home. There were ugly bullet wounds in his shoulder and his thigh. He was faint enough from pain and loss of blood, but his hurt was not mortal. His two constables—the fine brave escort he took with him everywhere—had fired into the darkness and run away, like the cowards they were, into the bog. Mr. Keene was taken to the Hall by the police, on his own car. The two runaway constables were found late that afternoon—or was it the next day?—tied up and gagged in an old roofless cabin a mile away. One of them had a paper pinned on his breast, with this printed on it:

> *These are not worth an honest man's powder and lead.*
> *I have taken the spalpeens'[20] guns, to put them to better use*
>   *very soon.*
>   —Captain Moonlight

You can guess that this threw Balbarry into wild excitement. Since the old Whiteboy days, no like thing had happened in our part. The very name "Captain Moonlight" was new to us. But, faith, we caught its meaning as if it had been the name of

20. The Irish term "spalpeens" is used here in its meaning "rascals" or "worthless n'er-do-wells." The signature "Captain Moonlight" was used by the Whiteboys (see note 10) on demand notes and the like left following moonlight raids.

a brother. And after that, when any two of us met, though we may have talked of mangel-wurtzels[21] or the price of bacon, the glance in each man's eye was asking of the other: whom do you suspect? Yet if all the parish had known of a certainty, on my soul I don't think there's a man who would have told.

Clap upon this attempt on Keene's life came other things from the same hand. Mangan's hay-ricks, that he'd the same as stolen from the Daunts, were fired a night or two later and burned to the very sod. Lonely houses where lived men with gun licenses were visited nightly, for miles around, and stripped of their weapons and ammunition by bands of masked men. Warnings were mysteriously served on the village tradesmen, who supplied the Hall, to stop it. More police were sent here, and a whole company of soldiers, but that had no effect on "Captain Moonlight" save to make him bolder.

Now I said to myself from the outset: the Farleys and Dalys, who lived in the Glen, are just the divvils for this business. There had been some elections out there, and a girl had been cut with a police bayonet, and an old woman, put out of her house, had died of lung trouble. I knew the wild boys of that neighborhood too well to suppose they would take these things calmly. And then there came into my mind the old stories of the hidden caverns, of the dark secret approaches to the underground river known only to these Gaelic descendents of the Terryalts and Ribbonmen.[22] In particular, I hit upon Turlogh Farley, a big-shouldered, square-jawed, choleric young daredevil, as the probable leader of this masked crew. It was more like his work than any other's I could think of, yet I knew that he could hardly write his name, and "Captain Moonlight" wrote, or rather

21. A type of beet fed to livestock.

22. The Terryalts and Ribbonmen were direct action secret societies. Like the Whiteboys, they carried out night raids against certain landlords from the eighteenth into the nineteenth century. The Ribbonmen were a specifically Catholic underground organization.

printed, like a clerk. This it was that puzzled me, for the school-master had never been able to make anything of the rough and stubborn material sent to him from the Glen. There was no solitary scholar among them all. Still, I made no doubt, after a few days, that the Moonlighters were the boys of the Glen.

I judged that others had reached this same conclusion, for I thought I could see that the Farleys and Dalys, when they came to town, were treated with more consideration by the villagers than formerly. They were big, strapping fellows, the men-folk of both of these families, who had lived side-by-side and inter-married since Cromwell's day. They were civil with me but no more, because for long before my time there had been a standing quarrel between them and the priest of this parish about the marriage of cousins. More than once I had put down my foot, in the early years when I knew no better, and they had been to the trouble of getting a dispensation over my head, through the influence of somebody at Dublin; I could never learn who. But they came to mass, in an irregular way, and to confession when they liked, once in a dog's age or so, and I had learned to give them their own gait and get on as quietly with them as I could. So I was not in the way to learn much from them, even if I had wanted to know. And, my word for it, I was in two minds as to whether I did or not.

Well, to cut a long story short, the knowledge came upon me like a burst of a thunder cloud one night late in March. Were I to live a thousand years, I should never forget that night!

I had been in the evening to the widow Carew's to show her a letter fresh from my friends in Baltimore, the contents of which troubled my mind. The letter itself said only that after young Mitchel Daunt learned of his parents' deaths through the newspapers, he disappeared. That was all that could be told about him. But with the letter came a clipping from an American paper, describing the dark picture of the boat and the maddened man and the dead woman. This much was well done, but it was a terrible mistake and libel which followed. The reporter had picked up some idle gossip among the silly old women of Balbarry, and on the strength of this built the wicked and foolish story that poor, spotless, loving, true-hearted Maev Carew had helped bring this terrible calamity upon the parents of her affianced husband, by learning to love young Lord Concannon better. This monstrous folly had been put into print—her name wasn't given, but no one could doubt who was meant—and Mitchel had read it in the same minute with the awful news from his own home!

Well, I talked it over with the Widow Carew that evening. I was for saying nothing of it to Maev, but the mother, with her proud, fine knowledge of her daughter's strength and spirit, said "yes," and I showed the crazy falsehood to the girl. She bore it better than either of us older people had been able to do.

"Mitchel will know that is false," she said confidently. "He will know that I would have given my life to save his father and mother, as I would give it to save him. How can you dream that he would doubt me?"

She put this question to me almost sternly, standing very erect and looking down upon me as I sat by the hearth, with a proud glow in her eyes. I grew confused under this glance.

"But you don't realize," I made answer, "this abominable thing is put forth here in type as a fact. The newspaper gives it as truth."

"But it is a lie! You know it is a lie," she replied, as if there was nothing more to be said.

"Ah yes, *I* know to be sure," I answered. "So does every decent soul in Balbarry. But Mitchel was not in Balbarry. We must remember that. And he read this false story given thus circumstantially for truth."

"Mitchel would know better," was her reply, and I forbore to say more.

We talked—the mother and I—for a little longer, the maiden sitting with her work opposite me and looking abstractedly into the fire. She kept her face calm, so long as I was there, and her voice was steady enough in the few remarks she added to our conversation. But when I had bid them good night, and had gone as far as the outer door, I heard a rustle of dresses, a sudden suppressed burst of sobbing, and then a plaintiff, faltering moan of anguish.

"Oh, why has he not written to me, mother? Why? Why?"

I looked back and saw against the faint candlelight the tall figures of the two women melted, as it were, into one. Maev was weeping bitterly in her mother's arms.

I came back here with a more leaden load than ever on my mind. I went to bed, and, strangely enough, was not kept awake by the trouble. But I had evil dreams, one after the other, and in the last of these nightmares there was a tremendous outburst of noise and tumult, which seemed to shake the very earth. The shock awakened me and, after an instant of maze, connected itself with a furious pumping which now began again on my street door. I sprang out of bed—I am highly accustomed to these night-wakings—and lifted the window to call out that I would be ready in a minute or two if I was really needed.

At my door stood two constables with rifles slung over their backs, one of them with a flaming torch. In the background, other figures were visible.

"Come out as quick as you can!" the fellow with the torch growled brusquely. "The doctor's away, and you're wanted without delay."

Under other circumstances, I might have resented this rude tone, but something like an intuition restrained me. I hurried on my clothes and hastened to join the policemen in the street. They started down the road at a swinging pace, one on each side of me, as if I had been a prisoner. At first they were not disposed to answer the questions I put, as we strode along in the red-flambeau light, but eventually they let me know this much, which I daresay was all they knew.

There had been, an hour or so before, some sort of attempt at violence up at the Hall, but whether to kill the Honorable Michael Considine or blow up the house or capture its guns was uncertain. At any rate, it had been interrupted by the police, and chase had been given to the marauders. They had scattered and disappeared in the darkness, but one had been pursued by the sound of his flying footsteps into the village and down the main street. There, trace of him for the moment was lost, but another patrol coming up the street, a few minutes later, had suddenly caught sight of the dark figure of a man gliding furtively along in the shadow of the houses. They had called to him to halt, and when at this he started to run they had fired and brought him down. He was lying at the police barracks, nearby where he fell. He was a stranger to the police. He had been picked up insensible and had remained so. He seemed to be seriously wounded. This, in brief, was the story.

I went into the big room of the barracks—which, to that hour, had been an alien and unknown place to me—and made my way through the cluster of constables, standing about, to the table in the center of the chamber. There, lying flat on his back with blanched face, closed eyes, a blood-drenched shirt, and disordered, shabby apparel, lay Mitchel Daunt!

V

I'm tiring you, so I'll hurry over what followed. It was not a fatal wound that the man had, but it was more than a month before he was able to get on his feet and was fit to be moved to the jail at T——, our assize town.[23] During this month, I saw him nearly

23. Outside the Four Courts in Dublin, there were six assize circuits, one of which was the Connaught circuit. Assize courts, part of a system established

every day, and, to be fair to them, the police left us alone together very often indeed.

It's the first talk I had with him that showed me his mind. He had been sensible for two or three days back, but I had had no chance to speak with him privately. When the opportunity came, it was a week after the terrible night, and I sat by his bedside in the little room where he had been moved by the doctor's orders, for want of an infirmary. He kept his eyes closed, but I knew he was awake and thinking.

"Mitchel," I said to him, "what in the name of glory have you been at? It isn't only that you've got penal servitude in front of you, when you're well enough to even sit up in the dock, but you've broken the heart of the noblest girl in all Connemara. Shame on you, I say, for such a divvil's deed as that!"

He opened his eyes at this and looked me square in the face.

"My father," he said in a weak voice, but with a bitter look in his eyes—"my father—rest his soul—died cursing her, and when they hang me, I'll do the same!"

"Give me you for the fool of the earth," said I in a heat at his perversity. "You read that in a lying newspaper. Where had your sense gone that you believed such wicked rubbish? Your father, poor, good man, was raving and out of his mind when he uttered those meaningless words—as mad as a March hare—but you— what excuse is there for you? It's not lunacy that's in your head but a divvil! Nobody will hang you but penal servitude you will get as sure as my name's Thomas. And there's the poor, white-faced colleen at home, weeping her eyes out for shame, with her life ruined as hopelessly as yours is. Out on you for working such mischief!"

---

in the seventeenth century, sat twice a year in designated towns for trials of a more serious kind than the ones overseen by local magistrates. It is not clear why Frederic uses dashes here following the capital "T." Tuam, of course, comes to mind as a possibility.

"She's ashamed, is she?" he snarled back at me, trying to lift himself in his bed. "Doesn't that prove what I say? Oh yes! She's a lady now, and so she's ashamed. When she was only a simple Irish girl, with honest Irish blood in her veins, she'd have gloried in what's been done to avenge the wrongs and hardships and the murders we've suffered. But it shames her now!"

He gave a scornful laugh at this and fell back on his pillow. Weak and helpless as he was, I could have beaten him on the head with my fists.

"Listen to me, you omadhaun!" I demanded. "There's no word of truth in what you say. She's not changed, save as your own follies and unworthiness have changed her from a happy, light-hearted girl to a sad one. She never ceased to love you much better than you deserve. More's the pity, she loves you still. God knows if I could talk her out of it, I'd wear my tongue down to the roots to do it, but her heart is too full of you. As for shame, it's not for the hurt to Keene or the burning of Mangan's ricks she blushes. It's for *you*—for your weakness in believing her false and for your cowardly sneaking home again and hiding unbeknownst to her—her, who'd go through purgatory for you, with a smiling face."

"But she'd cease smiling, I'm bound, when she met my father and mother there," replied he, with no relenting in his eyes.

"You're no Christian," I said. "I'll do penance for that you come from my parish. If there's a heathen left inside a white skin the world over, you're that same."

"I am the son of Patrick Daunt and of Margaret, his wife," was the answer he made me. He shut his eyes at that, and soon I left him.

It was some time before I had the patience to speak civilly to him again, though I called almost daily to see him; such talks as we had were for the most part like what I've already described. Once he asked me—perhaps it was the first day—who else had been arrested, and I told him no one, and he seemed glad of the news. But more than that, we never spoke of the night occurrences or of the doings of Captain Moonlight. I knew well enough who that gentleman was now, and he knew I knew, and there was nothing to be said. He had a fever the second week and then a long spell of weakness before he could sit up. Once I asked him if he would like to see Maev, but he shook his head fiercely.

To tell the truth, my mind was more concerned with the good women at my cousin's house. The sadness there was on that threshold I can't describe to you; it was too mournful. Whenever I could spare the time from my duties—and I fear the parish rightly thought that was a deal too often—I used it to go to this stricken house. Hour by hour, we would sit by the hearth—we three—and say scarcely a word to one another. The mother had begun to age from that very night, and the poor colleen moved about the house like a ghost, pale and silent. I gave them news each day of Mitchel—now that he was worse, now that he was better. They listened eagerly always, but they seemed to understand why I told them nothing of my conversations with him. They never once asked what he said.

So the month went by, and Maev drooped daily as Mitchel recovered. A lawyer came from Cork to offer to defend the young man, but Mitchel scarcely thanked him and replied that what defense was to be made he would make himself. A crown solicitor came down from T—— and got up the case against Mitchel. The police had come under such rebuke for not finding the other Moonlighters that they were all the more active in getting evidence against this one prisoner they had captured. There was not much, in truth, except the fact that he had been found long after midnight in the streets of Balbarry, trying to avoid observation. But on this were to be hung so many inferences that we all felt there was little hope of his escape. And if he was convicted, it meant at least twelve years' penal servitude. Poor Mitchel! Poor Maev!

The day came at last when he was to be taken to the jail at T——, to stand his trial at the spring assizes. My temper had softened toward him these last few days, bitterly as I chafed at his wrongheaded folly, and I went to the barracks to see him start. He was let out, still very pallid and weak but with hand-cuffs on for the first time, and helped up to the car, where three constables, well armed, also sat. I wrapped around his knees and feet a rug I had brought, and I am sure there were tears in my eyes—for all his bad behavior—when I shook his hand and blessed him, and the car drove off.

I watched it go down the street—the road being so muddy that they couldn't drive fast. The windows of Widow Carew's were all closed, the shutters tight drawn. Mitchel turned his head away as he passed the house.

This was on a Monday, and it was thought that his case would come up by Thursday. It was my intention to go to T—— for the trial, and I had made my arrangements accordingly so that I might start on Wednesday. Judge my surprise when, on the previous day, Maev came here to the house and told me that she would accompany me. I could foresee nothing but pain and anguish for her in this and tried to dissuade her, but she was resolute.

Then I thought it my duty to use authority.

"You shall not go!" I said.

"Ah, but Father Tom," she answered quite boldly, "if I have to go alone, still it won't turn me from going!"

I had never heard this tone in her voice before, and when I looked up, there was something new in her face as well. The color had gone out of it these many days, poor girl, but if it was as white as marble, it was as firm, too, now that I looked upon it. And in her eyes there was a strange kind of exultation—such a look as St. Cecilia might have had when she walked into the arena to meet the Lions.

With the glance she gave me—faith!—all my resolution died out. I could not pretend that I thought it wise, or even liked it, but I gave consent to her going. Her mother, it seems, had also tried to argue her out of the notion but had failed, as I did.

So Maev and I started out together, with my man, Jerry, here as driver and general guide and guard. It is a long day's ride, as you know, but during it all we barely spoke to each other. Jerry talked in plenty, never fear, and I answered him whenever he needed replies, but the girl sat silent, looking at nothing, with the same unreal, strange, martyr-like gaze in her eyes. And when we came into the town, found lodging in the hotel, had our dinner, and then parted for the night, it was all the same to her. The look, in fact, frightened me, and I slept badly—fearing more even for her than for Mitchel.

We were in the courtroom early next morning and saw the sour-looking, red-faced, old judge, in wig and snuffy gown, take his place; and the jury, a decent-appearing lot of men, all Protestants, mind, but still decent, file into the box; and then the poor devil of a prisoner, whose fate they had in their hands, was brought into the dock and allowed to sit, with two big constables beside him.

It was the first time Maev had laid eyes on him since his departure for America. I felt a shudder run through her frame as he entered; she leaned slightly against my shoulder and for a moment laid her hand on mine.

There was a great crowd in court, in the rear of the seats given privileged people, among whom we were. A murmur rose from them as Mitchel entered, walking feebly but with his handsome, curly head thrown proudly back and his eyes still aglow with defiance. I looked around, and it was like glancing over my own congregation—so many Balbarry folk were there among them. The sight made me feel less forlorn. Even the stalwart Dalys and Farleys, whom I picked out here and there in the throng, seemed like old friends. One of these, big Turlogh Farley, edged his way along till he stood pushed up against the rail of the bar, in front of everybody else, and close to the dock. He never once took his eyes off Mitchel.

The Crown produced its case. Witnesses were called to prove the attempt upon Balbarry Hall, the circumstances of the capture of the prisoner, his antecedents and cause for enmity against the Honorable Michael Considine, his mysterious presence in Ireland in hiding for nearly six weeks (for they had traced the ship he came over in), the fact that the outrages near Balbarry began within a week after he landed, and so on. The evidence went very smoothly, for the police witnesses had been well drilled, and almost before we realized what was happening, the case for the Crown had closed.

Then Mitchel Daunt stood up to speak in the absence of a lawyer for himself. He said that really there was nothing proved, except that he was on the street late at night, but going toward the Hall instead of away from it. As for the rest, it was mere surmise. It was not for an accused man to prove his innocence. The Crown must prove guilt, and much more of the same sort. Mitchel spoke well, or rather looked finely as he spoke, but really there was not much in his words. Somehow I had hoped for more, and a kind of chill seized me when I saw him sit down. If this was all, God help him!

"What witnesses do you call?" asked the old judge, severely, for he had made it plain at the beginning that he hated to have prisoners undertake their own defense.

"Your Lordship, I have none!" said Mitchel, rising to his feet again. He made as if he would speak further, when a most startling interruption came.

Maev Carew had risen swiftly beside me and stood leaning

forward in visible excitement. She was trembling from head to foot and clasping the top of the seat before her for support.

"My Lord! My Lord!" she called out in a shrill, strong voice that seemed not Maev's at all—"I am a witness! Let me be sworn!"

The sound of her own words appeared to reassure her, for she ceased trembling and stood erect. There had been a moment's confusion upon her rising, but all was now as still as death. Every eye was fastened on her, and the people, crowded in the rear, pushed forward noiselessly, with bated breath.

"Order in the court!" called out somebody. I put my hand upon Maev's arm with some vague notion of getting her to sit down, but she shook off my touch and stood more erect than ever.

"Who are you?" asked the judge, not so unpleasantly this time. He added, "If you are not called, you cannot testify."

Maev turned toward the dock where Mitchel stood with his arms folded, looking fixedly at the floor, and piteously she entreated him—

"Mitchel, dear, it's for my sake you're doing this. You shall not murder yourself for me—you must not. For the love of God, Mitchel, call me as your witness!"

The judge looked at the beautiful girl who stood before him, and at the Crown lawyers, one or two of whom had risen to interpose, and at the prisoner, who still scowled moodily downward and had never turned to the girl. Finally, his lordship, waving aside one of the Crown lawyers who started to say something, asked Mitchel sharply: "Do you call this young woman for your witness?"

Mitchel still did not look in our direction. He hesitated for a long minute. Then he answered: "No!" and sank into his seat

What devil's mystery was in this all, I wondered. I remember in that moment of stupefaction catching sight of Turlogh Farley's face, and it too was all blank amazement. He was staring at Maev with his mouth open and his eyes like saucers.

The judge cut into the mystified silence by again addressing Mitchel: "You seem a very obstinate and perverse young man," he said, "whatever else you are. Since in your self-assurance you have rejected counsel, the court is in duty bound to guard your interest for you. Swear the witness!"

It was all like a dream to me. I could not realize that what I heard and saw was actually happening. Maev left my side, walking straight as a queen, and went to the witness box and took the oath. Then, as Mitchel would ask her no questions or even look at her, the judge acted as a lawyer himself and put the queries to her. She told him her name, her age, and her residence, and when he asked: "What are you to the prisoner?" she looked bravely around then spoke out so all could hear: "I am his promised wife."

"Go on!" said the judge, "Tell your story your own way. That will be best."

Try and imagine how we listened! The throng in that courtroom hardly breathed, so eager were they for every word. As for myself, I seemed to have all at once grown foolish and paralytic. I could do nothing but sit there in numbness and stare at the girl.

"My Lord!" said Maev, still with the strange altered voice, "Mitchel Daunt could not have been at the Hall that night! I can swear to that! He was not there."

"Tell me more," said the judge. "Where was he then—of your own knowledge?"

Two bright spots of pink came into the colleen's cheeks, showing almost like blood against the pallor of her skin. She looked straight at Mitchel, hesitated for a moment, and then answered: "It's hard for a girl to say—the thing—here before everybody—but *he was with me*! It's to save my reputation that he makes no defense. He was after leaving my house when they arrested him—the house is but a step or two from where he was taken."

The girl told this amazing story boldly, without faltering, and without ceasing to watch Mitchel. The crowd breathed a long, deep sigh, half relief, half bewilderment. The turn things had taken lifted us all off our feet, and more wonders were coming.

Mitchel had looked swiftly around at Maev when she made her astounding declaration. He seemed for a moment dumb-founded by it. Then, as she finished, he sprang up excitedly and waved his arms toward the judge.

"My Lord, it is not true!" he shouted. "Don't believe her! If it was my dying breath, I'd swear it was not true! I'd swear that—that—"

He broke off like this, looked wildly around for a second, with his face working in a strange way, and then fell like a clod of earth to the floor in a dead swoon.

There was a scene of great confusion that followed. Faith, I think I was near fainting myself. All I remember was the con-stables picking Mitchel up, still senseless, starting to carry him out, and being stopped by the judge. It seemed his presence was needed, for his lordship decided that the trial had gone far enough. And then the jury stood up, words were exchanged, and the first thing I knew, Turlogh Farley gave a great "hurroo!" and the Dalys and Farleys in back took it up, and other spectators shouted, and then, as the constables carried the fainting man out, there were loud commands for "order in the court," and there was no order.

Mitchel Daunt had been acquitted!

Oh yes—one thing more I remember. While the cheering was still in my ears, Maev Carew came to me. The people sepa-rated to let her pass, and even those who were cheering for joy drew back·so that she might not touch them.

She came straight to me. Her face was as gray as ashes, and on it was a look of terrible, heart-crushing weariness. She took me by the arm.

"Come," she said. And oh! the hard, dry misery of her tone! "Let us go back. There is no more for me to do here." And so we went. And that's the story.

VI

The good priest had been much affected during the latter portions of this long and remarkable recital, and I confess myself to having followed it with not a little emotion. Father Carew turned now and busied himself with filling his pipe and mixing some punch from the kettle that had been steaming and singing on the crane over the fire. An interval of silence ensued, which I at last broke by saying: "I felt that there must have been some such tremendous tragedy as this, from the wild, startled look Maev gave me when I met her in the convent—or perhaps I haven't told you that I saw her."

The priest stopped short in his amiable task, with a spoonful of sugar poised in the air, and looked curiously at me. I thought he even smiled, inwardly.

"And what convent might that be, pray?" he asked, still with spoon in hand.

"Why, at K——, where we stopped at noon today. Father McNamara—that's his name, I think—showed us over the convent and in the lace room, where a young nun was showing us the embroideries and laces. I happened to mention to him that I knew you and Mrs. Carew and her daughter, and at the sound of the names this nun turned and gave me—heavens!—what a look!—and left the room. It wasn't until she'd gone that I recognized her as Maev herself."

I had not been mistaken. The good priest *was* chuckling to himself.

"Sure, that wasn't Maev at all, at all," he said, with a smile at my error in his gray eyes. "Maev and Mitchel were married here in my very church, by me, not two months after the trial." He spoke more seriously as he went on: "It would not have been easy for them to live here, for the price she paid for her lover's freedom seemed too dear to our highland notions. They are living in Detroit, Michigan, and from the letters, they're doing very well, indeed. And there is a boy called Thomas, after me. A fine lad he is, too, I'm credibly informed."

"But I could have sworn it was Maev! How could I so mistake? And why should she have started and looked at me so strangely, at the mention of your names?"

"It's simple enough," replied Father Carew. "The nun you saw was Maev's elder sister, who took the veil at K—— nine years or so ago. She's much like Maev in face and eyes but"—he illustrated the conclusion to his sentence by tapping his forehead significantly with his finger—"not so like here."

"In fact," he went on, half musingly, "that sister in the convent got more trouble out of the whole affair than anyone else. Though the Widow Carew was much shocked at first, and grieved herself into illness and old age, still she's come to think differently now—her mother's heart led her that way—and now she dreams of nothing but of going next year to America, to end her days with Maev and Mitchel. But the nun—faith! Nothing will convince her but that Maev's soul is lost to all eternity."

"Evidently you don't entirely share that view," I remarked, taking the glass he handed me. "Arrah! What do *you* think?" said Father Carew.

Chapter 2

THE LADY OF MUIRISC

I

At Three Castle Head

Even with Kate, potential Lady of Muirisc though she was, this fashion of a hat was novel.[1] It seemed only yesterday since she had emerged from the chrysalis of girlhood with a shawl over its head, and heaven only knows what abysses of ignorant shyness and stupid distrust inside that head. And, alas, it seemed but a swiftly oncoming tomorrow before this new freedom was to be lost again and the hat exchanged forever for a nun's veil.

"The Lady of Muirisc" is excerpted from Frederic's *The Return of the O'Mahony*. Hereafter, bracketed ellipses […] indicate the removal of material not relevant to "The Lady of Muirisc" as an independent story. See editor's introduction for more details.

1. Part 1 of the story occurs at Three Castle Head, close to Kate's village at the southwest tip of the Ivehagh Peninsula near the open Atlantic. Part 2 takes place near Mount Gabriel, close to Schull and Roaring Water Bay on the peninsula's eastern side. While the other place names in this story are authentic geographical ones, Kate's home village—Muirisc—appears to be fictional, although there is a townland named Murreagh—Muirisc in Irish—in the far north of the peninsula near Durrus (Muintervara), and Frederic may have drawn the name "Muirisc" from there. The year, as per the time scheme in *The Return of the O'Mahony*, is around 1875. Kate is the potential "Lady" of Muirisc in the local O'Mahony line, but the inheritance and the ladyship are very modest. And if she were to become a nun—as she is being pushed to—she would forgo the inheritance.

If Kate had known natural history better, she might have likened her lot to that of the Mayfly, which spends two years underground in its larva state hard at work preparing to be a fly, and then, when it at last emerges, lives only for an hour, even if it that long escapes the bill of the swallow or the rude jaws of the trout. No such simile drawn from stony-hearted nature's tragedies helped her to philosophy. She had, perhaps, a better refuge in the health and enthusiasm of her own youth.

In the company of her ancient servitor, Murphy, she was spending the pleasant April days in visiting the various ruins of the O'Mahonys on Ivehagh. Many of these she viewed now for the first time, and the delight of this overpowered and kept down in her mind the reflection that perhaps she was seeing them all for the last time as well.

"But how, in the name of glory, did they get up and down in their boats, Murphy?" she asked at last, strolling farther out toward the edge to catch the full sweep of the cliff front, which rises abruptly from the beach below, sheer and straight, a clear, three hundred feet.[2]

"There's never a nearer landing place, thin, than where we left our boat, a half-mile beyant here," said Murphy. "Faith, miss, 'tis the belafe they went up and down be the aid ʼ ʼhe little people. 'Tis well known that, on windy nights, there dᴜ be grand carrin's-on hereabouts. Sure in the lake forninst us it was that Kian O'Mahony saw the enchanted woman with the shape on

2. That the people of this coast could land boats on the rocky shore with its wild seas and bring their goods and gear up sheer cliffs still provokes amazement. "It is conceivable," Frederic writes, "that they had rope ladders, and even windlass appliances for raising and lowering boats over this terrifying abyss.... But one has only to see the native fishermen of Cape Clear, who alone retain the characteristics that were probably common to all the coastmen of medieval Munster, run under heavy burdens like monkeys up a bare face of seemingly perpendicular rock to realize that ladders and tackle may not have been needed at all." Frederic, "Coast of White Foam," 5.

her of the horse and died of the sight. Manny's the time me own father related to me that same."[3]

"Oh, true, that *would* be the lake of the legend," said Kate. "Let us go down to it, Murphy. I'll dip me hand for wance in water that's really bewitched."

The girl ran lightly down the rolling side of the hill and across the rock-strewn hollows and mountains which stretched toward the castellated cliff. The base of the third and most inland tower was washed by a placid freshwater pond covering an area of several acres and heavily fringed at one end with rushes. As she drew near, a heron suddenly rose from the reeds, hung awkwardly for a moment with its long legs dangling in the air, and then began a slow, heavy flight seaward. On the moment Kate saw another even more unexpected sight—the figure of a man on the edge of the lake with a gun raised to his shoulder, its barrel following the heron's clumsy course. Involuntarily, she uttered a little warning shout to the bird, then stood still, confused and blushing. Stiff-jointed old Murphy was far behind.

The stranger had heard her, if the heron had not. He lowered his weapon and for a moment gazed wonderingly across the water at this unlooked-for apparition. Then, with his gun under his arm, he turned and walked briskly toward her. Kate cast a searching glance backward for Murphy in vain, and her intuitive movement to draw a shawl over her head was equally fruitless. The old man was still somewhere behind the rocks, and she had only this citified hat and even that not on her head. She could see that the advancing sportsman was young and a stranger.[4]

3. The lake at Three Castle Head situates a local version of the Lady of the Lake legend. It was said to be, and still is, haunted by a ghost woman who sometimes emerged from its waters in the guise of a horse; the sighting of her was considered deadly. The legend is referred to in "The Path of Murtogh" as well.

4. This scene, as noted in the introduction here, is a clear reference, and probably an homage, to the well-known story "A White Heron" by Frederic's American localist contemporary Sarah Orne Jewett. In that story, Sylvie comes

He came up close to where she stood and lifted his cap for an instant in an offhand way. Viewed thus nearly, he was very young, with a bright, fresh-colored face and the bearing and clothes of a gentleman. "I'm glad you stopped me, now that I think of it," he said, with an easy readiness of speech. "One has no business to shoot that kind of bird, but I'd been lying about here for hours, waiting for something better to turn up, till I was in a mood to bang at anything that came along."

He offered this explanation with a nonchalant half-smile, as if confident of its prompt acceptance. Then his face took on a more serious look, as he glanced a second time at her own flushed countenance.

"I hope I haven't been trespassing," he added, under the influence of this revised impression.

Kate was, in truth, frowning at him, and there were no means by which he could guess that it was the effect of nervous timidity rather than vexation.

"'Tis not my land," she managed to say at last, and looked back again for Murphy.

"No—I didn't think it was anybody's land," he remarked, essaying another propitiatory smile. "They told me at Goleen[5] that I could shoot as much as I liked. They didn't tell me, though, that there was nothing to shoot."

The young man clearly expected conversation, and Kate, stealing further flash studies of his face, began to be conscious that his manner and his talk were not especially different from those of any nice girl of her own age. She tried to think of something amiable to say.

"'Tis not the sayson for annything worth shooting," she said, and then wondered if it was an impertinent remark.

---

upon a young man, a hunter, who is in search of a white heron. Jewett's tale in effect shadows this one—both involve a young rural girl's coming of age.

5. Town on the east coast of the peninsula, north of Crookhaven.

"I know that," he replied. "But I've nothing else to do just at the moment, and you can keep yourself walking better if you've got a gun, and then, of course, in a strange country there's always the chance that something serious *may* turn up to shoot. Fact is, I didn't care so much after all whether I shot anything or not. You see, castles are new things to me—we don't grow 'em where I come from—and it's fun to me to mouse around among the stones and walls and so on. But this is the wildest and lonesomest thing I've run up against yet. I give you my word, I'd been lying here so long, watching those mildewed old towers there and wondering what kind of folks built 'em and lived in 'em, that when I saw you galloping down the rocks here—upon my word I half thought it was all a fairy story. You know, the poor people really believe in that sort of thing here. Several of them have told me so."

Kate actually felt herself smiling upon the young man.

"I'm afraid you can't always believe them," she said. "Some of them have deludhering ways with strangers—not that they mane any harm by it, poor souls!"

"But a young man down below here, today," continued the other—"mind you, a young man—told me solemnly that almost every night he heard with his own ears the shindig kicked up by the ghosts on the hill back of his house, you know, inside one of those ringed Danes's forts, as they call 'em. He swore to it, honest Injun."

The girl started in spite of herself, stirred vaguely by the sound of this curious phrase with which the young man had finished his remarks. But nothing definite took shape in her thoughts concerning it, and she answered him freely enough: "Ah, well, I'll not say he intinded desate. They're a poetic people, sir, living here alone among the ruins of what was once a grand country and now is what you see it, and they imagine visions to thimselves. 'Tis in the air, here. Sure, you yourself"—she smiled again as she spoke—"credited me with being a fairy. Of course," she added, hastily, "you had in mind the legend of the lake, here."

"How do you mean—legend?" asked the young man in frank ignorance.

"Sure, here in these very waters is a woman with the shape of a horse, who appears to people, and when they see her, they—they die, that's all."

"Well, that's a good deal, I should think," he responded, lightly. "No, I hadn't heard of that before, and, besides, you—why—you came down the hill, there, skipping like a lamb on the mountains, not a bit like a horse."

The while Kate turned his comparison over in her mind to judge whether she liked it or not, the young man shifted his gun to his shoulder, as if to indicate that the talk had lasted long enough. Then she swiftly blamed herself for having left this signal to him. "I'll not be keeping you," she said, hurriedly.

"Oh, bless you—not at all!" he protested. "Only I was afraid I was keeping *you*. You see, time hangs pretty heavy on my hands just now, and I'm tickled to death to have anybody to talk to. Of course, I like to go around looking at the castles here, because the chances are that some of my people sometime or other helped build them. I know my father was born somewhere in this part of County Cork."

Kate sniffed at him.

"Manny thousands of people have been born here," she said with dignity, "but it doesn't follow that they had anything to do with these castles."

The young man attached less importance to the point.

"Oh, of course not," he said carelessly. "All I go by is the probability that, way back somewhere, all of us O'Mahonys were related to one another. But for that matter, so are all the Irish who—"

"And are *you* an O'Mahony, thin?"

Kate was looking at him with shining eyes, and he saw now that she was much taller and more beautiful than he had thought before.

"That's my name," he said simply.

"An O'Mahony of County Cork?"

"Well, personally, I am an O'Mahony of Houghton County, Michigan, but my father was from around here, somewhere."

"Do you hear that, Murphy?" she asked, instinctively turning to the faithful companion of all her out-of-door life. But there was no Murphy in sight.

Kate stared blankly about her for an instant before she remembered that Murphy had never rejoined her at the lakeside. And now she thought she could hear some vague sound of calling in the distance, rising above the continuous crash of the breakers down below.

"Oh, something has happened to him!" she cried, and started running wildly back again. The young man followed close enough to keep her in sight and at a distance of some three hundred yards came up to her as she knelt beside the figure of an old peasant seated with his back against a rock.

Something had happened to Murphy. His ankle had turned on the stone, and he could not walk a step.

"Oh, what's to be done *now*?" asked Kate, rising to her feet and casting a puzzled look about her. "Sure me wits are abroad entirely."

No answer seemed forthcoming. As far inland as the eye could stretch, even to the great crown of Dunkelly, no sign of human habitation was to be seen. The jutting headland of the Three Castles on which she stood—with the naked primeval cliffs; the roughly scattered boulders framed in scrub-furze too stunted and frightened in the presence of the sea to venture upon blossoms; the thin ashen-green grass blown flat to earth in the little sheltered nooks where alone its roots might live—presented the grimmest picture of desolation she had ever seen. An undersized sheep had climbed the rocks to gaze upon the intruders—an animal with fleece of such a snowy whiteness that it looked like an imitation baa-baa from a toy shop—and Kate found herself staring into its vacuous face with sympathy, so helplessly empty was her own mind of suggestions.

"'Tis two Oirish miles to the nearest house," said Murphy, in a despondent tone. Kate turned to the young man and spoke wistfully: "If you'll stop here, I'll go for help," she said.

The young man from Houghton County laughed aloud.

"If there's any going to be done, I guess you're not the one that'll do it," he answered. "But, first of all, let's see where we stand exactly. How did you come here, anyhow?"

"We rowed around from—from our home—a long way distant in that direction," pointing vaguely toward Dunmanus Bay, "and our boat was left there at the nearest landing point, half a mile from here."

"Ah, well, *that's* all right," said the young man. "It would take an hour to get anybody over here to help, and that would be clean waste of time, because we don't need any help. I'll just tote him over on my back, all by my little self."

"Ah—you'd never try to do the likes of *that!*" deprecated the girl.

"Why not?" he commented, cheerfully—and then, with a surprise that checked further protest, she saw him tie his game-bag round his waist so that it hung to the knee, get Murphy seated up on the rock against which he had leaned, and then take him bodily on his back, with the wounded foot comfortably upheld and steadied inside the capacious leathern pouch.

"Why not, eh?" he repeated, as he straightened himself easily under the burden; "why he's as light as a bag of feathers. That's one of the few advantages of living on potatoes. Now you bring along the gun—that's a good girl—and we'll fetch up at the boat in no time. You do the steering, Murphy. Now, then, here we go!"

The somber walls of the Three Castles looked down in silence upon the strange procession as it filed passed under their shadows—as if the gulls that wheeled above and about the moss-grown turrets described the spectacle later to the wraiths of the dead-and-gone O'Mahonys and to the enchanted horse-shaped woman in the lake, there must have been a general agreement that the parish of Kilmoe had seen never such another sight before, even in the days of the mystic Tuatha de Danaan.[6]

The route to the boat abounded to a disheartening degree in rough and difficult descents, and even more trying was the frequent necessity for long *détours* to avoid impossible barriers of rock. Moreover, Murphy turned out to be vastly heavier than he had seemed at the outset. Hence the young man, who had freely enlivened the beginning of the journey with affable chatter, gradually lapsed into silence; and at last, when only a final ridge of low hills separated them from the strand, he confessed that he would like to take off his coat. He rested for a minute or two after this had been done, and wiped his wet brow.

"Who'd think the sun could be so hot in April?" he said. "Why, where I come from, we've just begun to get through sleighing."

"What is it you'd be slaying now?" asked Kate, innocently. "We kill our pigs in the late autumn."

The young man laughed aloud as he took Murphy once more on his back.

"Potato-bugs, chiefly," was his enigmatic response.

She pondered fruitlessly upon this for a brief time, as she followed on with the gun and coat. Then her thoughts centered themselves once more upon the young stranger himself, who seemed only a boy to look at, yet was so stout and confident of

6. Deities of pre-Christian Ireland.

himself, and had such a man's way of assuming control of things, and doing just what he wanted to do and what needed to be done.

Muirisc did not breed that sort of young man. He could not, from his face, be more than three or four and twenty—and at that age all the men she had known were mere slow-witted, shy, and awkward louts of boys, whom their fathers were quite free to beat with a stick, and who never dreamed of doing anything on their own mental initiative, except possibly to "boo" at the police or throw stones through the windows of a boycotted shop. Evidently, there were young men in the big unknown outside world who differed immeasurably from this local standard.

Oh, that wonderful outside world, which she was never going to see! She knew that it was sinful and godless and pressed down and running over with abominations, because the venerable nuns of the Hostage's Tears[7] had from the beginning told her so, but she was conscious of a new and less hostile interest in it, all the same, since it produced young men of this novel type. Then she began to reflect that he was like Robert Emmett, who was the most modern instance of a young man that the limits of convent literature permitted her to know about, only his hair was cut short, and he was fair, and he smiled a good deal, and—

And lo, here they were at the boat! She woke abruptly from her musing daydream.

The tide had gone out somewhat and left the dingy stranded on the dripping seaweed. The young man seated Murphy on a rock, untied the game-bag and put on his coat, and then in the most matter-of-fact way tramped over the slippery ooze to the boat, pushed it off into the water, and towed it around by the chain to the edge of the little cove, whence one might step over its side from a shore of clean, dry sand. He then, still as if it were all a matter of course, lifted Murphy and put him in the bow of the boat and asked Kate to sit in the stern and steer.

7. Religious order that has schooled Kate in Muirisc.

"I can talk to you, you know, now that you're sitting there," he said, with his foot on the end of the oar seat, after she had taken the place indicated. "Oh—wait a minute! We were forgetting the gun and bag."

He ran lightly back to where these things lay upon the strand, and secured them; then, turning, he discovered that Murphy had scrambled over to the middle seat, taken the oars, and pushed the boat off. Suspecting nothing, he walked briskly back to the water's edge.

"Shove her in a little," he said, "and I'll hold her while you get back again into the bow. You mustn't think of rowing, my good man."

But Murphy showed no sign of obedience. He kept his burnt, claw-shaped hands clasped on the motionless, dipped oars, and his eager, bird-like eyes fastened upon the face of his young mistress. As for Kate, she studied the bottom of the boat with intentness and absently stirred the water over the boat-side with her fingertips.

"Get her in, man! Don't you hear?" called the stranger, with a shadow of impatience, over the six or seven feet of water that lay between him and the boat. "Or *you* explain it to him," he said to Kate; "perhaps he doesn't understand me—tell him I'm going to row!"

In response to this appeal, Kate lifted her head and hesitatingly opened her lips to speak—but the gaunt old boatman broke in upon her confused silence: "Ah, thin—I understand well enough," he shouted, excitedly, "an' I'm thankful to ye, an' the longest day I live I'll say a prayer for ye—an' sure ye're a foin grand man, every inch of ye, glory be to the Lord—an' it's not manny wud a' done what you did this day—and the blessin' of the Lord rest on ye; but—" here he suddenly dropped his high, shrill, swift-chasing tones and added in quite another voice—"if it's the same to you, sir, we'll go along home as we are."

"What nonsense!" retorted the young man. "My time doesn't matter in the least—and you're not fit to row a mile—let alone a long distance."

"It's not with me fut I'll be rowin'," replied Murphy, rounding his back for a sweep of the oars.

"Can't *you* stop him, Miss—eh—young lady!" the young man implored from the sands.

Hope flamed up in his breast at sight of the look she bent upon Murphy, as she leaned forward to speak—and then sank into plumbless depths. Perhaps she had said something—he could not hear, and it was doubtful if the old boatman could have heard either—for on the instant he had laid his strength on the oars, and the boat had shot out into the bay like a skater over the grassy ice.

It was a score of yards away before the young man from Houghton County caught his breath. He stood watching it—be it confessed—with his mouth somewhat open and blank astonishment written all over his ruddy, boyish face. Then the flush upon his pink cheeks deepened, and a sparkle came into his eyes, for the young lady in the boat had risen and turned toward him, and was waving her hand to him in friendly salutation. He swung the empty game-bag wildly above his head in answer, and then the boat darted out of view behind a jutting ridge of umber rocks, and he was looking at an unbroken expanse of gently heaving water—all crystals set on violet satin, under the April sun.

He sent a long-drawn sighing whistle of bewilderment after the vanished vision.

Not a word had been exchanged between the two in the boat until after Kate, yielding at the last moment to the temptation that had beset her from the first, waved that unspoken farewell to her new acquaintance and saw him a moment later abruptly cut out of the picture by the intervening rocks. Then she sat down again and fastened a glare of metallic disapproval, so to speak, upon Murphy. This, however, served no purpose, as the boatman kept his head sagaciously bent over his task and rowed away like mad.

"I take shame for you, Murphy!" she said at last, with a voice as full of mingled anguish and humiliation as she could manage to make it.

"Is it too free I am with complete strangers?" asked the guileful Murphy, with the face of a trusting babe.

"'Tis the rudest and most thankless old man in all West Carbery that ye are!" she answered sharply.

"Luk at that now!" said Murphy, apparently addressing the handles of his oars. "An' me havin' the intention to burr'n two candles for him this very night!"

"Candles is it! Murphy, once for all, 'tis a bad trick ye have of falling to talking about candles and 'Hail Marys' and such holy matters, whenever ye feel yourself in a corner—and be sure the saints like it no better than I do."

The aged servitor rested for a moment upon his oars, and, being conscious that evasion was of no further use, allowed an expression of frankness to dominate his withered and weather-tanned face.

"Well, miss," he said, "an' this is the truth I'm tellin' ye—'twas not fit that he should be sailin' in the boat wid you."

Kate tossed her head impatiently.

"And how long are you my director in—in such matters as these, Murphy?" she asked with irony. [...]

II

Near the Summit of Mount Gabriel

A vast sunlit landscape under a smiling April sky—a landscape beyond the uses of mere painters with their tubes and brushes and camp-stools, where leagues of mountain ranges melted away into the shimmering haze of distance, and where the myriad armlets of the blue Atlantic in view, winding themselves about their lovers, the headlands, and placidly nursing their children, the islands, marked as on a map the coastwise journeys of a month—stretched itself out before the gaze of young Bernard O'Mahony, of Houghton County, Michigan—and was scarcely thanked for its pains.[8]

The young man had completed four-fifths of the ascent of Mount Gabriel, from the Dunmanus side,[9] and sat now on a moss-caped boulder, nominally meditating upon the splendors of the panorama spread out before him, but in truth thinking deeply of other things. He had not brought a gun, this time, but had in his hand a small, brand-new hammer, with which, from time to time, to point the shifting phases of his reverie, he idly tapped the upturned sole of the foot resting on his knee.

From this coign of vantage he could make out the white walls and thatches of at least a dozen hamlets, scattered over the space of thrice as many miles. Such of these as stood inland he did not observe the second time. There were others, more distant, which lay close to the bay, and these he studied intently as he mused, his eyes roaming along the coastline from one to another in baffled perplexity. There was nothing obscure about them, so far as his vision went. Everything—the innumerable croft-walls dividing the wretched land below him into holdings; the dark umber patches where the bog had been cut; the serried layers of gray rock sloping transversely down the mountain-side, each with its crown of canary-blossomed furze; the wide stretches of desolate plain beyond, where no human habitation

8. It is two days after Bernard's having met Kate at Three Castle Head and he, like her, is continuing a walking tour. It may seem that they cover extraordinary distances, but the peninsula is rather narrow, and aside from bog land and rocky areas, fairly easily traversed. Mount Gabriel, a rugged high-point from which vistas open out in all directions, was the site of Stone Age copper mines.

9. Dunmanus Bay is to the west of the Ivehagh Peninsula.

could be seen, yet where he knew thousands of poor creatures lived, all the same, in moss-hidden hovels in the nooks of the rocks; the pale sheen on the sea still farther away, as it slept in the sunlight at the feet of the cliffs—everything was as sharp and distinct as the picture in a telescope.

But all this did not help him to guess where the young woman in the broad, black hat lived.

Bernard had thought a great deal about this young woman during the forty-eight hours which had elapsed since she stood up in the boat and waved her hand to him in farewell. In a guarded way he had made inquiries at Goleen, where he was for the moment domiciled, but only to learn that people on the east side of the peninsula are conscious of no interest whatever in the people reputed to live on the west side. They are six or eight Irish miles apart, and there is high land between them. No one in Goleen could tell him anything about the beautiful dark young woman with a broad, black hat. He felt that they did not even properly imagine to themselves what he meant. In Goleen the young woman are not beautiful, and they wear shawls on their heads, not hats.

Then he had conceived the idea of investigating the west shore for himself. On the map in his guidebook this seemed a simple enough undertaking, but now, as he let his gaze wander again along the vast expanse of ragged and twisted coastline, he saw that it would mean the work of many days.

And then—then he saw something else—a vision which fairly took his breath away.

Along the furze-hedge road which wound its way up the mountainside from Dunmanus and the South, two human figures were moving toward him, slowly, and still at a considerable distance. One of these figures was that of a woman, and—yes, it was a woman!—she wore a hat—as like as could be to that broad-brimmed, black hat he had been dreaming of. Bernard permitted himself no doubts. He was of the age of miracles. Of course it was *she*!

Without a moment's hesitation he slid down off his rocky perch and seated himself behind a clump of furze. It would be time enough to disclose his presence—if, indeed he did at all—when she had come up to him.

No such temptation to secrecy besets us. We may freely hasten down the mountainside to where Kate, walking slowly and pausing from time to time to look back upon the broadening sweep of land and sea below her, was making the ascent of Mount Gabriel.

Poor old Murphy had been left behind, much against his will, to nurse and bemoan his swollen ankle. The companion this time was a younger brother of the missing Malachy, a lumpish, silent "boy" of twenty-five or six, who slouched along a few paces behind his mistress and bore the luncheon basket. This young man was known to all Muirisc as John Pat, which was by way of distinguishing him from the other Johns who were not also Patricks. As it was now well on toward nine centuries since the good Brian Boru ordained that every Irishman should have a surname, the presumption is that John Pat did possess such a thing, but feudal Muirisc never dreamed of suggesting its common use. This surname had been heard at his baptism; it might be mentioned again upon the occasion of his marriage, though his wife would certainly be spoken of as Mrs. John Pat, and in the end, if he died at Muirisc, the surname would be painted in white letters on the black wooden cross set over his grave. For all the rest he was just John Pat.

And medieval Muirisc, too, could never have dreamed that his age and sex might be thought by outsiders to render him an unsuitable companion for Miss Kate and her wanderings over the countryside. In their eyes, and in his own, he was a mere boy, whose mission was to run errands, carry bundles, or do whatever else the people of the castle bade him do; in return for which they, in one way or another, looked to it that he continued to live, and even on occasion, gave him an odd shilling or two.

"Look now, John Pat," said Kate, halting once more to look back; "there's Dunbeacon and Dunmanus and Muirisc beyant, and, may be if it wasn't so far, we could see the Three Castles, too; and when we are at the top, we should be able to see Rosbrin and the White Castle and the Black Castle and the strand over which Ballydesmond stood, on the other side, as well. 'Tis my belafe no other family in the world can stand and look down on seven of their castles in one view."

John Pat looked dutifully along the coastline as her gesture commanded, and changed his basket into the other hand, but offered no comment. [...]

Kate, in vast surprise, turned at the very first sound of a strange voice. A young man had risen to his feet from behind the furze hedge, close beside her, his rosy-cheeked face wreathed in amiable smiles. She recognized the wandering O'Mahony from Houghton County, Michigan, and softened the rigid lines into which her face had been startled, as a token of friendly recognition.

"Good morning," the young man added, as a ceremonious afterthought. "Isn't it a lovely day?"

"You seem to be viewing our country hereabouts with great completeness," commented Kate, with a half-smile, not wholly free from irony. There really was no reason for suspecting the accidental character of the encounter, save the self-conscious and confident manner in which the young man had, on the instant, attached himself to her expedition. Even as she spoke, he was walking along at her side.

"Oh, yes," he answered, cheerfully, "I'm mixing up business and pleasure, don't you see, all the while I'm here—and really they get so tangled up together every once in a while, that I can't tell which is which. But just at this moment—there's no doubt about it whatever—pleasure is right bang-up top."

"It *is* a fine, grand day," said Kate, with a shade of reserve. The frankly florid compliment of the Occident was novel to her.

"Yes, simply wonderful weather," he pursued. "Only April, and here's the skin all peeling off from my nose."

Kate could not but in courtesy look at this afflicted feature. It was a short, good-humored nose, with just the faintest and kindliest suggestion of an upward tilt at the end. One should not be too serious with the owner of such a nose.

"You have business here, thin?" she asked. "I thought you are looking at castles—and shooting herons."

He gave a little laugh, and held up his hammer as a voucher.

"I'm a mining engineer," he explained: "I've been prospecting for a company all around Cappagh and the Mizen Head, and now I'm waiting to hear from London what the assays are like. Oh, yes—that reminds me—I ought to have asked before—how is the old man—the chap we had to carry to the boat? I hope his ankle's better."

"It is, thank you," she replied.

He chuckled aloud at the recollections which the subject suggested.

"He soured on me, right from the start, didn't he?" The young man went on. "I've laughed a hundred times since, at the way he chiseled me out of my place in the boat—that is to say, *some* of the time I've laughed—but—but then lots of other times I couldn't see any fun in it at all. Do you know," he continued, almost dolefully, "I've been hunting all over the place for you."

"I've nothing to do with the minerals on our lands," Kate answered. "'Tis a thrushtee attinds to all that."

"Pshaw! I didn't want to talk minerals to *you*."

"And what thin?"

"Well—since you put it so straight—why—why, of course—I

wanted to ask you more about our people, about the O'Mahonys. You seemed to be pretty well up on the thing. You see, my father died seven years ago, so that I was too young to talk to him much about where he came from, and all that. And my mother, her people were from a different part of Ireland, and so, you see—"

"Ah, there's not much to tell now," said Kate, in a saddened tone. "They were a great family once, and now are nothing at all, wid poor me as the last of the lot."

"I don't call that 'nothing at all,' but a jug full," protested Bernard, with conviction.

Kate permitted herself a brief cousinly smile.

"All the same, they end with me, and afther me comes in the O'Dalys."

Lines of thought raised themselves on the young man's forehead and ran down to the sunburned nose.

"How do you mean?" he asked, dubiously.

"Are you—don't mind my asking—are you going to marry one of that name?"

She shrugged her shoulders, to express repugnance at the very thought.[10]

"I'll marry no one; laste of all an O'Daly," she said, firmly. Then, after a moment's hesitation, she decided upon a further explanation. "I'm goin' to take me vows at the convint within the month," she added.

Bernard stared open-eyed at her.

"I-gad!" was all he said. [...]

"But say, you don't mean it, do you—*you* going to be a nun?"

10. Cormac O'Daly is a villainous usurper in the novel *The Return of the O'Mahony*. He has intruded himself into the affairs of Muirisc to the point that he runs things, and has lately married Kate's none-too-astute mother. Kate's confinement to the convent will suit his purposes well as she is the last of the Muirisc O'Mahony line. The people of the hamlet are unaware—and so is he at this point—that Bernard is the legitimate O'Mahony in line to inherit the Muirisc Castle and its surroundings.

She looked at him through luminous eyes, and nodded a grave affirmative.

Bernard walked for a little way in silence, moodily eying the hammer in his hand. Once or twice he looked up at his companion as if to speak, then cast down his eyes again. At last, after he had helped her to cross a low, marshy stretch at the base of a ridge of gray rock, and to climb to the top of the boulder—for they had left the road now and were making their way obliquely up the barren crest—he found words to utter.

"You don't mind my coming along with you," he asked, "under the circumstances?"

"I don't see how I'm to prevint you, especially wid you armed with a hammer," she said, in gentle banter.

"And I can ask you a plain question without offending you?" he went on; and then, without waiting for an answer, put his question: "It's just this—I've only seen you twice, it's true, but I feel as if I'd known you for years, and, besides, we're kind of relations—are you going to do this of your own free will?"

Kate, for answer, lifted her hand and pointed westward toward the pale-blue band along the distant coastline.

"That castle you see yonder at the bridge—" she said, "it was there that Finghin, son of Diarmid Mor O'Mahony, bate the MacCarthys wid great slaughter, in Anno Domini 1319."

The two young people, with John Pat and the basket close behind, stood at last upon the very summit of Gabriel—a wild and desolate jumble of naked rocks piled helter-skelter about them, and at their feet a strange, little, circular lake, which in all the ages had mirrored no tree or flowering morning rush or green thing whatsoever, but knew only of the clouds and of the lightning's play and of the gathering of the storm demons for dissent upon the homes of men. [...]

The while John Pat stripped the basket of its contents, and spread them upon a cloth in the mossy shadow of an overhanging boulder, the two by a common impulse strolled over to the eastern edge of the summit.

"Beyond Roaring Water Bay[11] the O'Driscoll Castles begin," said Kate. "They tell me they're poor trifles compared wid ours."

"I like to hear you say 'ours,'" the young man broke in. "I want you to keep right on remembering all the while that I belong to the family. And—and I wish to heaven there was something I could do to show how tickled to death I am that I do belong to it!"

"I have never been here before," Kate said in a musing tone, which carried in it a gentle apology for abstraction. "I did not know there was anything so big and splendid in the world."

The spell of this mighty spectacle at once enchanted and oppressed her. She stood gazing down upon it for some minutes, holding up her hand as a plea for silence when her companion would have spoken. Then, with a lingering sigh, she turned away and led the slow walk back toward the lake.

"'Twas like dreaming," she said with gravity; "and a strange thought came to me: 'Twas that this lovely Ireland I looked down upon was beautiful with the beauty of death; that 'twas the corpse of me country I was taking a last view of. Don't laugh at me! I had just that feeling. Ah, poor, poor Ireland!"

Bernard saw tears glistening upon her long, black lashes, and scarcely knew his own voice when he heard it, in such depths of melancholy was it pitched.

"Better times are coming now," he said. "If we open up the mines we are counting on it ought to give work to at least two hundred men."

She turned sharply upon him.

"Don't talk like that!" she said, in half command, half entreaty. "'Tis not trade or work or mines that keeps a nation alive

11. The bay is on the Cork coast west of Baltimore and east of the Mizen Peninsula.

when 'tis fit to die. One can have them all, and riches untold, and still sink wid a broken heart. 'Tis nearly three hundred years since the first of the exiled O'Mahonys sailed away yonder [...] and so for centuries the stream of life has flowed away from Ireland wid every other family the same as wid ours. What nation under the sun could stand the drain? [...] So"—her great eyes flashed proudly through the tears—"don't talk of mines to me! 'Tis too much like the English!"

Bernard somehow felt himself grown much taller and older as he listened to this outburst of passionate lamentation, with its whiplash end of defiance, and realized that this beautiful girl was confiding it all to him. He threw back his shoulders, and laid a hand gently on her arm.

PART II

Chapter 3

IN THE SHADOW OF GABRIEL

1550

The cool maiden breath of dawn lay upon the coast, and a light, so soft and irresolute that all shadows seemed a part of it, covered the rocks and dormant waters and the dim brown bulk of rising land beyond with an even-spread mantle, mist-colored and motionless as sleep. A thousand cormorants and gulls stood silent in thick gray lines upon the ridges of the islets in the cove, as if they had been charmed to stone. The slow wash of the tide on the strand's edge, restrained by this small spell of the great hush, lifted the loose weight of seaweed and sucked at it cautiously, with a stealthy, low-drawn murmur like a sigh.

Suddenly, over the high, rounded spine of Mount Gabriel, a bar of red flame flared into the sky, and the face of everything was on the instant changed. The pale upper slopes of the archangel's mountain darkened in a frown where they hung menacingly above the woods. Depths of umbra shade burned themselves into the bases of the tall crags lining the sides of the cove, as glancing pink lights picked out their veins of marble higher up. The outer waters of the bay sulked from drab to purple, and thence to black, shrinking away from the red morning toward the somber masses of clouds in the west. The swell on the beach growled and flung up through the drift vexed splashes of foam, which flushed crimson at the sight of the sunrise and hissed at it as they fell again. All at once, as upon a signal, the fisher-fowl rose from their night perch, a confused and tumultuous mob, splashing and wheeling in frenzy of their long hunger, and splitting the air with sinister screams. A new bad day was born.

Around the steep northern headland, in this perturbed moment of awakening, there slipped into view a small boat, bellying low in the water and bearing six men. It was a coracle, rudely fashioned of skins strained tight upon bent withes, and four men, kneeling with faces to the bow, pushed it forward with short paddles. Two others stood behind and, like the workers, kept a rapt gaze of inquiry upon the shore they neared. The boat crept along the nearer cliff wall of the inlet, as if in its furtive course even that measure of companionship with things of substance was welcome. When a landing place had been found, and the boat drawn up against the drifting beach at the end, the two men on their feet leaped out; the four with the paddles gave no sign of following.

"Oh then, Turlogh, son of Fineen, why would we not be remaining here to guard the boat?" urged the oldest of them. "We are simple men, and it is no good place for us."[1]

---

1. The youthful Turlogh has recently inherited the chieftainship of Dunbeekin on the death of his father, Fineen. His men, while loyal, have great misgivings about Turlogh's strength, judgment, and fitness for leadership. He has not the cut of a warrior but is thoughtful and given to reading. The Irish practice regarding succession to chieftainship was tanistry, not primogeniture—the fittest male inherited leadership. There must be no more promising male available in the family at this point than the unpromising Turlogh. He is not without spirit and determination, however, and a certain enlightenment—he will not leave unexplored, as his father did, the matter of an alleged beast that haunts a wood in his territory. Accompanied by some of his men and by a monk, Brother Florentius, he has come to seek out whatever is in the wood. The monk is a stranger arrived at Dunbeekin only two days earlier, but his assurances of religious protection against what dwells in the wood have reassured Turlogh in his determination to explore the mystery of the monster.

Turlogh looked at them and bent his brows. He was the youngest of the party, a tall stripling of thin frame, with narrow shoulders and a pale, grave face. The spear in his hand, upon which he leaned as he stood, and the short, broidered tunic and mantle of smooth cloth he wore were in the fashion of a warrior: but his eyes were framed for the timid glances of a girl. He strove to look sternly out of them.

"You will always be disputing, old Cumara," he said. "Come out of that, all of you!"

The others bent troubled glances upon the water at the sides of the boat and stirred their paddles aimlessly. A low murmur of protest spread without words among them.

"It is not fit for us to go," reiterated their spokesman, doggedly.

"And you would stop at your ease here," cried the young man, "and see me pass out of your sight into the little oakwood of the strand, and know that maybe I will come into the alder hollow itself! My father would have thrown you out of your boat and piled stones upon you under the water and left you for the devil crabs to dig you out. And it is in me to do the same, too!"

Cumara made a show of concern upon his countenance, but his eyes grinned.

"That would be the way of your father, rest him in glory," he assented, "and without doubt it would be your way also, for in boldness and mighty deeds you are his own son—"

"Ah, Cumara," broke in the young man, "you know that is not your opinion. You have no proper fear of me—you or the others. You mock when my back is turned. I will not be suffering it any more. I have as good a heart of courage in me as my father, and I will put the weight of anger upon you as he would have done. Come out of the boat!"

Turlogh's men, however, in the grasp of superstition, are disinclined to follow him and the monk inland.

"Your father," returned the other, nodding his long, horse-like head to point the words, "would never have wished to go to the little oakwood of the strand. (This was *derreennatra* in their Irish, and the alder hollow was *coomfarna*.) He would not come into this water at all, not by any means, and he would not bid those who belonged to him to come either. And we are very sad now to see ourselves here in this boat, because it is already too far for us to go in search of our own harm, and yours, it is more than enough that we have done."

"Listen, Cumara," said Turlogh, more gently—"I am not of great strength, like my father, and I have not your years, but there is pride in me nonetheless. And I take shame to myself to be lord in Dunbeekin and chief of the people of the O'Mahony Cruachan,[2] and live like a blind slave, not knowing what would be in that oak thicket, or in the alders of the glen beyond. It is nothing to me that my father did not choose to come here. I do not have his mind. I have my own mind, and my thoughts bid me to come here and go where I have the right to go, in my own territory, and see all that meets my eyes. I cannot be sure that there is any harm here, because I have not seen it, and no one has seen it."

"It is too terrible for our eyes to behold," said a man in the boat who had not spoken before.

"He runs on his four bones through the alders too swiftly to be seen," cried another.

"He has a beard of feathers instead of hair," groaned the third, "and his lips are of horn, like a bird's beak, and the smallest wave of his hand will send the blood bursting from your ears."

Old Cumara made a last appeal. "If we have not seen him, we know what he does. Oh, that is very well known. Children that he has overlooked wither in their bones and die of the sickness. The

---

2. The meaning of "cruachan" here appears to be something like "tribe," but it is not clear. *Cruchan* was the name of the ancient royal site of Connaught.

horses on the mountain come to the edge of the alders, and he feeds them, and their bellies swell and rot, and their hooves drop off. In the full of the moon, he climbs to the height of the hill, and he looks down on Dunbeekin, and if his *beim-sol* catches so much as the glimpse of a cow in the bawn, she gives blood next morning and no milk.[3] Oh, then, Turlogh, son of Fineen, be said by us and come into the boat, and the friar with you, and we will be going to our own place. It is Cumara who begs you to do that."

The young man shook his bare head. "I will go into the wood," he said between his teeth, "and I will go without any cowards at my heels to make my back cold with their fears. And if I come upon anyone who is able to stop me, or do me mischief, then let him be lord in Dunbeekin and not me."

With a sudden gesture, he turned to his companion, standing on the wet litter by his side. "Have you fears also?" he demanded.

It was a short, sturdily made, dark man, in years somewhat older then Turlogh, who answered. He had thrown the cowl of his brown monk's habit back upon his shoulders, and the sunlight shone upon the broad grayish patch of his tonsure and on the round face full of composure and self-confidence. He gathered up the long chain depending from his girdle and grasped the wooden cross at its end in his hand.

"How should I have fears?" he asked. "Have I not told you I would go with you? Do I not possess powers over demons and false spirits?"

Turlogh knit his brows, and his face twitched in a brief hesitation. Then, without a word or a backward glance at the boat,

3. The bawn is an enclosure for cattle, close by or attached to a house or castle. "*Beim-sol*" or "*sol-bheim*" is a flash of light, a thunderbolt, or beam—here the monster's gaze. "The Irish use 'sol-bheim' for a flash of light—eminently lightning. And 'sol-beim' is strictly a stroke from the eye, but, in the usual acceptation, a bewitching by it" (John Whitaker, *The History of Manchester, 1775*, vol. 2, 248).

he lifted his spear and started across the drenched reach of sea-weed to gain dry land. At the third stride, his foot slipped on the treacherous ooze, and he fell with violence upon the sharp rocks. The monk watched him rise and brush the clinging slime from his mantle, and touch the bruised cut upon his knee, with attentive eyes.

"It will be your warning, Turlogh, son of Fineen!" shouted Cumara from the boat.

A sustained, low mutter of distant thunder vibrated through the air as the old kerne's voice died away.[4] The sunlight had grown yellow and gave the bleached pebbles and shells on the dry strand beyond a brazen hue. The monk, still pausing with a thoughtful face, looked to the west. Vast walls of gloomy clouds curled up-ward over the face of the sky, enfolding the mountain of Beara in their coils.[5] Below them the waters of Dunmanus were as ink.

"A great storm will be blowing in from the sea," he said, and as he spoke a streak of lightning flashed in their eyes.

"Oh, then, forked lights and thunder on Christmas Day!" clamored Cumara. "'Twas never seen before! Be warned, my O'Mahony."

"I will not look behind!" cried Turlogh. Pointing the way with his spear, he strode forward. The monk, with a shrug of his shoulders, followed.

A hundred paces inland, through a cleft in the barrier of tall, gray cliffs, the ascent began. As they entered this narrow glen, to the gaunt steep sides of which misshapen and stunted oaks, scarce the bigness of furze bushes, clung with tops drawn back-

---

4. Kerne—of Irish derivation. Referred to an Irish foot soldier and came to be used in English to refer to a rustic, rough-hewn peasant, sometimes—as may be the case here—with the further implication of rascal. See OED.

5. The neighboring Beara Peninsula can be seen to the west from Mount Gabriel. For a view of contemporary life there, see "On the Beara Peninsula: Written in Stone" by Leanne O'Sullivan, *New Hibernia Review* 17, no. 3 (Autumn 2013): 9–14.

ward from the sea, the sunlight failed. A last dismayed wail of entreaty from the men in the boat mingled with the clatter of the first large raindrops and hail on the rocks.

"I will not at all turn!" repeated Turlogh, stubbornly. He clambered up the oblique ridges of boulders, pushing aside with a spirited hand the sprawling oak bows from his path. The monk followed, lifting his gown as he came and springing lightly from ledge to ledge.

The thicket closed upon them; the storm burst. Not much rain fell through the matted canopy of twisting branches low overhead. The trees writhed and ground their limbs together, shrieking as the tempest smote them. The splitting of dry wood made an endless crackle in their ears as the men went on, and the higher oaks rocked and swung their arms and cried to one another while they struck their gnarled, lesser neighbors down. A somber twilight reigned in these wilds depths—illumined now here, now there by momentary gleams of blue flame, which glided downward among the tree stems and left vistas of a midnight blackness veined by a fiery network of intertwined twigs and branches before Turlogh's eyes.

The young chieftain halted and drew back with a little, startled cry as a blinding ark of fire burst through the hanging mistletoe just before his face and quivered in zigzag lines among the creepers at his feet. He put a hand over his eyes and groped behind him with the other to touch the monk's gown.

"Yonder, under the ledge of rocks, we will be safer from the lightning," said the monk, still calm of voice. "I would not have you killed that way!"

With a hand on Turlogh's shoulder, he guided him to one side, where a dark recess beneath the shelf of jutting boulders offered refuge. The young man moved as one dazed, stumbling over the strewn litter of the storm, and sank upon his knees in the sheltered gloom under the rooks.

"I would be saying some prayers," he murmured, "if you would tell me the fit ones."

Then a spasm of shuttering shook his thin frame. He lifted a livid face toward the standing monk, and his lips moved but made no sound. A frenzy of frightened inquiry dilated his eyes. A long-bodied dog, sleek-coated and drab of hue, with a flat head and broad, thick snout, had come suddenly to him out of the vague shadows and stood there thrusting his cold muzzle against Turlogh's knee and licking it.

He would have screamed but had no power save to gasp in his throat. The monk, stooping, beat the dog over the head with the cross, and it slunk off into the obscurity again as it had come, like a thing of no substance.

"You will be needing the prayers at a later hour," said the monk. He raised his voice to make it heard above the tumult of the blast sweeping past them.

Turlogh bit his teeth together and struggled against his weakness.

"I am not afraid in my heart!" he cried. "I would not suffer myself to turn back, no, not for the lordship of all Ivehagh. But my bones are like unwilling servants, and my bowels have the terror in them. But I am their master and now have no fears anymore." He strove to smile where he knelt and reached forth his hand for the spear he had dropped, and which the monk had picked up. "Tell me," he added, "would it have been known to you that so much evil would happen to us first?"

"Yet more will happen," returned the monk. He did not seem to note Turlogh's hand outstretched for the spear. "But you will be remembering," he went on, "I gave you a warning. It does not lie in your right to say the contrary."

There was something unusual in the voice Turlogh heard. He looked up more keenly at his companion.

"I would not be saying anything contrary to your words,

Brother Florentius," he said. The noise of the storm forced him to lift his voice as well. "You are a holy man, and you are a stranger to me, and you are my guest, and I would not dispute whatever you spoke. But it is not in my memory that you warned me of anything. It was you who came to Dunbeekin two days since and sat in my hall in the evenings and told your part of the tales, as a traveler is looked to do, and sang your songs when my bard had done. And your tales were bold and moving, and your songs stayed with me in my sleep, and these things warmed me toward you. And when the speech of my people fell upon this little oakwood of the strand and the altar hollow beyond, and they told of the man-witch who lived here, and ran like a wolf through the thicket, and had an eye to blast what he looked upon, and feathers to his beard instead of hair, it was you who left with scorn and put shame in me that I had never left likewise. And it was your word that on Christmas Day no fiends or unnatural powers could prevail against Christians who were after taking the blessed sacrament before sunrise. And it was your own word that you would come with me and go to the length of the oakwood and the hollow. And why should you be saying now that I dispute with you?"

A lull had fallen over the storm. The monk laughed but made no answer. This was not to Turlogh's liking.

"You say you gave me warning," he declared, putting his foot forward to rise. "And it is my reply that I cannot remember it. I have in my memory only your promise that if I saw malignant sights they should do me no harm. And I have seen you drive that terrible dog away with the stroke of your cross, and my mind is at ease. I have no complaint to make; only I do not know what you mean by your words about a warning."

The monk looked down at him, a mirthless smile playing on his shaven lips.

"You forget, then, my warning that if an O'Mahony met on

Christmas Day a chieftain of another sept sworn in blood feud against him and his people, it would be very bad—oh, very bad, indeed, for him."

"Oh, then I have some memory of what you are saying," returned Turlogh, in thought. "Those were your words, but they took no root in my mind. For our speech was of the enchantment, and the man-witch here—and—"

"And now it is of another matter!" called out the monk with a ring as of metal in his voice. On the instant, as Turlogh bent his knee to rise, the monk drove the spear into his right shoulder and thrust him fiercely backward, prone to the earth. The young man's legs were twisted under him, and the monk's sandaled foot crushed upon his breast. The thought of resistance died in his brain, for his arms lay limp, and he could not bring a hand to touch the spear.

"I know you are yourself the devil I was enticed here to defy," he said. The spearhead in his shoulder seemed to scorch his flesh, but his thoughts were the clearer for the anguish of it. He watched the studded jowl of the monk and looked to see a beard of feathers sprout upon it.

"I would not be wishing you to die in error," said the other, gazing with a measured wrath downward upon him. "I made you to take the blessed sacrament this day, that your soul might not perish, and I will not suffer you to go out of the world like a fool, in ignorance of why you are put away. I am no witch, or man enchanted. I am no devil. I am no monk. I am Fineen, son of Spollan, and on Christmas Day one year ago, I saw your father cleave my father's skull with a battle ax, while he lay hurt in his own bawn, and put the fire to Ballyfanisk, and drive our men over the cliff into the sea, and lay the shame of unclean beasts upon our women. And that is why I have come to keep this next Christmas Day with you, Turlogh, son of Fineen, and that is why you will be saying your prayers now."

Turlogh looked hard at him and remembered much.

"I was not one of the raid," he said, "but I would not be blaming you if you had come fairly to fight me and take my life. My father was a strong man, and he put his foot on the O'Dwyer's, and spoiled Ballyfanisk, and openly chased you all into the sea. And I would not blame him for that either. And you say that Spellan, your father, had his head split open with an ax. That would not be his worst luck. It was more evil fortune still for him to beget a son who would be a liar and a false guest."

The O'Dwyer tore open his gown at the breast with his free hand and cast it from him in a heap around his feet. His thick, supple form showed itself clad in the thick tunic of a warrior, and from shoulder to thigh he had a shirt of fine, linked iron chain work. Out of his belt he drew a long, thin dagger.

"The 'false guest' ate nothing under your roof that he did not bring with him," he said with sharpness. "The 'liar' warned you of your fate. And now there will be no further words. The storm is not spent, and there is a long day's journey over the mountain before me, and I will be taking with me your head wrapped in my gown. There is a short minute to you for your prayers."

A bold peal of thunder rolled over the face of the thicket and echoed from crag to crag along Mount Gabriel's flank. The blue lights glided again among the twigs overhead. Turlogh shut his eyes from them and sought a prayer. He could think only of Cumara and the men in the boat. They loved him, but they would never be minding him. They were not wrong. He was no right man to be a lord and chief over others. His brother, Conogher, was more fit. He would be knowing how to make them obey him. And sometime—somehow—he would be learning what black O'Dwyer had done. Maybe it would be the man-witch with the beard of feathers who would cause him to learn it. And now there was no time to find out if such a man-witch did run his ghastly course through the little oakwood and the alder hollow—or anything else whatever. The towers of Dunbeekin—he would not be seeing them again, or the black, fat herds in the bawns, or the pretty girls weaving their knots, or the fall of the evening shadows on the gray waters of Dunmanus—or any sight at all. He kept his eyes closed and bent his mind upon the familiar things they would never be looking at more, and waited.

But now there was a noise in the thicket which was not of the thunder or the rushing wind—a noise which burst suddenly close about him, of savage growls and curses, and crackling branches underfoot. The effort to take account of this gave Turlogh a moment's giddiness. The spear had been wrenched from a shoulder, and the deep pain of it racked and swayed his brain toward swooning. Then, getting his thoughts vaguely back from the threshold of death, he opened his eyes. On the instant, with a little cry of agony at the woe in his shoulder, he sat upright and stared white-faced and dumb with bewilderment.

What Turlogh had not seen before he sought the prayers that would not come was a dim, crouching figure in the darkness under the rocks, peering out from the obscurity with eyes alight, and, in imperceptible edgings forward, coming close to the back of the O'Dwyer.

What Turlogh's amazed eyes beheld were two powerful forms locked in a deadly grip, writhing, rocking, tugging in frenzied passion at each other, and tearing the soft mosses and forest carpet with their feet as they fought, within a pace of where he sat. A stick hurled upward from the ground struck him smartly on the cheek. He forced himself to rise to his feet and, with poised hands, thrust forward his face in the effort to see which was which of the two combatants. Even above the pain of his wound rose the violent lust to have a share in this furious struggle. But the light was low in these depths, and his eyes blurred. He shouted in his confused flutter of hope and fear, and one of the two embattled forms was thrust with violence against him. He reeled backward and caught at the rock to steady himself and had a moment's terror lest he should foolishly fall down where he stood.

It was another who fell with a forceful crash, and upon him plunged headlong the form of the victor. Turlogh saw blood on the leaves, and a blackened face turned upward among the roots with its eyes bursting forth at him in despairing horror. It was the face of the O'Dwyer, and Turlogh felt his foot itching to plant itself upon that face. He leaned against the rock instead and gulped something down that rose in his throat and shook off the faintness that was on him. Then there seemed to be more light, and he saw clearly.

A creature in the semblance of a man, half naked and, for the rest, clad in strange, discolored tatters of skins and rags, and with a savage mane of hair and beard growing in tufts and patches enveloping its head, knelt upon the breast of the O'Dwyer. It's sinewy hands, corded and stained to the likeness of some foul giant bird's talons, were clasped fiercely about the fallen man's throat. From its lips there came a hissing vile to hear.

Turlogh, looking, saw that the long-bodied, ashen-hued dog was there, too, close to his feet. He shuddered and pushed himself for support against the jutting boulder.

"Who are you?" he heard his own quavering voice ask.

The kneeling creature lifted its head and stared fixedly at Turlogh. The sense of mystery vanished on the instant. It was the face of an elderly omadhaun, vacant, smiling, furtive, pitiful. It nodded and grimaced under Turlogh's eye.[6]

"Have you no speech?" demanded Turlogh. He spoke freely now, as if to a strolling light-wit at his own gates.

"They beat me away with sticks and stones," said the simpleton. He spoke in a thin, muffled, squeaking voice, and it was not easy to comprehend his words. "They strike me and put the dogs after me, but someone is my father. It may be that in a year and

6. Omadhaun—simpleton, one mentally lacking.

a day he will come for me and feed me with white meats. I go to the head and look for him, because it is very bad for me here. He will be having a silk coat and gold pieces in his ears when he comes with the high tide."

Turlogh held up his hand to check the meaningless babble. The trees and the kneeling figure and the corpse swam before his eyes.

"Bear me down to the water's edge—to my boat!" he said abruptly.

The old man slowly withdrew his hands from the throat of the O'Dwyer.

"That gown it was that tripped him," he crooned, grinning, as he pointed to the monk's frock, still twisted about the dead man's legs, and with a sudden stray gleam of sense in his eyes. Turlogh's knees bent under him, and he clung with his elbows against the rock.

"Leave him, and bear me to my boat!" he groaned. And then blackness spread itself over all.

At night, in the little chamber beside the hall of Dunbeekin, the herb doctor and the bard stood together at the side of the low bed, and looked down at the pale, sleeping face of their young Lord. Old Cumara crouched behind them, in the shadows beneath the ring of fish-oil tapers against the wall.

"Oh, then, when the first cock crows," wailed the boatman, "the life will be out of him! The devil himself brought him out of the little oakwood and laid him on the strand and ran back, with a dog of hell at his heels. And we went alone on the strand, and we bore him to the boat with the mark of the devil's teeth torn into his shoulder. And the monk was not to be seen at all, the holy man! Oh, wirra, wirra! Why would it not be me instead?"

"Hsh-h!" muttered the herb doctor.

Turlogh had opened his eyes. He lifted himself on his left

elbow and looked around with a slow gaze, noting the faces about him and bringing his thoughts together, one by one. Then he smiled, and their hearts took joy, for there was no illness on him.

"Bring me food and drink now," he said, "and bid Culain the builder come to me in the morning. I will be raising a chapel in the little oakwood by the strand without delay, and I will dedicate it to St. Molaggi, the omadhaun."[7]

Cumara groaned, but the two others exchanged a glance and nodded.

"It will be to the memory of the holy man, the Friar, who went with you and did not return?" asked the bard.

Turlogh looked gravely at him and his companion, and then upward at the half-circle lights.

"Oh, then, it is you for the reading of men's thoughts!" he said to his bard and smiled again.

7. St. Molaggi or Molaga—seventh-century Cork saint. He was not himself an omadhaun, but a legend had it that his birth to aged parents was foretold by the "fool" Comhdhán Dá Chearda. See Pádraig O'Riain, *Dictionary of Irish Saints* (Dublin: Four Courts, 2011). Keeping quiet about the malevolent visit of the O'Dwyer, Turlogh lets lie the animosity and chain of revenge that would have ensued. This pacifism in Turlogh's character carries over thematically in the later story involving Turlogh, "The Truce of the Bishop."

Chapter 4

THE PATH OF MURTOGH

1579

A curse is laid on one long narrow strip of the sea, down in front of Dunlogher.

No matter how lifeless the sunlit air may hang above; no matter how silken-smooth the face of the waters nearest by, lifting themselves without a ripple in the most indolent summer swell, an angry churning goes always forward here. Disordered currents will never tire of their coiling and writhing somewhere underneath: the surface is streaked with sinister markings like black shadows, which yet are no shadows at all; and these glide without ceasing out and in among the twisted lines of grey-white scum, and everything moves and nothing changes, till Judgment Day. It has the name of the *Slighe Mhuircheartaigh* (spoken Shlee Vurharthee), or the Path of Murtogh.

Though 'tis well known that the grandest ling[1] and turbot and wonderful other big fishes lie swaying themselves in the depths of this wicked water, with giant crayfish and crabs to bear them company, the fishermen of Dunmanus and Goleen and Crookhaven, and even the strangers from Cape Clear, would not buy a soul from purgatory at the price of drawing a net through

1. Ling is a fish native to the waters off Ireland and other northern islands as far west as Iceland.

it. They have a great wish to please the buyers in the English ships, and the Scotch and Manx, oh, yes—but a creel of gold would not tempt them to meddle in "Murty's Path." They steer their boats far to one side and bless themselves as they pass, in the manner of their fathers and grandfathers before them.

These poor men, having not much of the Irish now, and not rightly understanding what their elders may have heard the truth of, say that this snake-like forbidding stretch wears its name from Murty *Oge* O'Sullivan. Their thought is that the uncanny boiling began in the wake of the English *Speedwell*, as the corpse of the vanquished privateer spun and twirled at her keel through the foam, on its savage last journey from Castletown to Cork. But it is enough to look down at this evil place, to see that the malediction upon it must be older than Murty *Oge's* time, which, in the sight of Dunlogher, was as yesterday. Why, men are living this year who talked with men who saw his head spiked over South gate. There were no great curses left unused in Ireland at so late a day as his. And again, would it be the waters of Dunlogher that would tear themselves for an O'Sullivan?[2]

No, the curse threads back a dozen lives behind poor Murty *Oge*. The strange currents weave and twine, and the greasy foam spreads and gathers, gathers and spreads, in the path of another, whose birthright it was that they should baptize him. The true tale is of Murty the Proud, or if you will have his style from the Book of Shull—Murtogh *Mordha*[3] O'Mahony, chief in Dunlogher. And his time is not so distant, in one way, as men take account of years. But in another it is too remote for any clear vision, because the "little people" of the old, fearful kind had left every other part of Ireland, and they were just halting

---

2. That is, Dunlogher is in O'Mahony territory, not O'Sullivan. Three Castle Head (where Kate first meets Bernard O'Mahony in "The Lady of Muirisc") was "Dunlogher" in the sixteenth century.

3. "Mordha" means "noble."

together for a farewell pause in Dunlogher, by reason of its being the last end of the land, and their enchantments fanned up
a vapor about Murty *Mordha* to his undoing. And it is as if that
mist still rose between us and his story.

|

When the sun began to sink out of sight, down behind the sea,
two men stood on the edge of the great cliff of Dunlogher, their
faces turned to the west.

The yellow flame from the sky shone full in the eyes of Murtogh, and he held his huge, bare head erect with boldness, and
stared back at it without blinking. His companion, a little, shriv-
eled old man, whom he held by the arm, had the glowing light
on his countenance as well, but his eyelids were shut. He bent
himself against his chief's thick shoulder and trembled.

"Are we to the brink itself?" he asked; his aged voice shook
when he spoke.

"Here, where I stand, when I would grip you, and hold you
forth at the length of my arm, and open my hand, you would
fall a hundred fathoms in the air." Murtogh's free arm and hand
made the terrible gesture to fit his words, but he tightened his
protecting clasp upon the other and led him back a few paces.
The old man groaned his sigh of relief.

"It is you who are the brave nobleman, Murty," he whispered
admiringly. "There is none to equal your strength, or your grand
courage, in all the land. And the heart of pure gold along with it!"

Murtogh tossed his big head, to shake the twisted forelock
of his hair to one side. "I looked straight into the sun at noon
on St. John's Day," he said, quietly, with the pride of a child. "If
it were a hundred times as bright, I would look at it and never
fear for my eyes. I would hold my own son out here, stretched
over the abyss, and he would be no safer in his bed. Whatever I
wished to do, I would do it."

"You would—oh, you would!" assented the old man, in tones of entire sincerity.

The chieftain kept his eyes on the skyline, beneath which, as the radiance above deepened, the waters grew ashen and coldly dark. Musing, he held his silence for a time. Then, with abruptness, he asked: "What age were you, Owny Hea, when the McSwineys put out your eyes? Were you strong enough to remember the sun well?"

"I was of no strength at all," the other whimpered, the tragedy of his childhood affecting his speech on the instant. "I was in my mother's arms. There were the men breaking in through the wall, and the kine bellowing outside, and my father cut down; and then it was like my mother drew her cloak tight over my head—and no one came ever to take it off again. I forget the sun."

Murtogh nodded his head. "I will go to Muskerry someday," he said in a kindly way. "I cannot tell when, just now; but I will go, and I will burn and desolate everything for six miles around, and you shall have a bag for your harp made of eyelids of the McSwineys."

Old Owny lifted his sightless face toward his master and smiled with wistful affection. "Ah, Murty, dear," he expostulated, mildly, "it is you who have the grand nature; but think, Murty— I am a very old man, and no kin of yours. It is fifty years since the last man who took my eyes drew breath. If you went now, no living soul could tell what you came for, or why the great suffering was put upon them. And, moreover, the O'Mahonys Carbery have wives from the McSwineys these three generations. No feud lies now."

The lord of Dunlogher growled sharply between his teeth, and Owny shrank further back.

"How long will you be learning," Murtogh demanded, with an arrogant note in his voice, "that I have no concern in the

O'Mahonys Carbery, or the O'Mahonys *Fonn-Iartarach*, or any other? I do not take heed of Conogher of Ardintenant, or Teige of Rosbrin, or Donogh of Dunmanus, or Donal of Leamcon. I will give them all my bidding to do, and they will do it, or I will kill them and spoil their castles. You could not behold it, but you have your song from the words of others: how last year I fell upon Donogh *Bhade*, and crushed him and his house, and slew his son, and brought away his herds. His father's father and mine were brothers. He is nearer to me in blood than the rest, yet I would not spare him. I made his Ballydevlin a nest for owls and bats. Let the others observe what I did. I am in Dunlogher, and I am the O'Mahony here, and I look the sun in the face like an eagle. Put that to your song!"

The sound came to them, from the walled bawn and gateways beyond the Three Castles, a hundred yards behind, of voices in commotion. The old bard lifted his head, and his brow scored itself in lines of listening attention. If Murtogh heard, he gave no sign, but gazed again in meditation out upon the vast waste waters, blackening now as the purple reflections of the twilight waned.

"Blind men have senses that others lack," he remarked at last. "Tell me, you, does the earth we stand on seem ever to you to be turning round?"

Owny shuddered a little at the thought which came to him. "When you let me out beyond here, and I felt the big round sea-pinks under my feet, and remembered they grew only on the very edge—" he began.

"Not that," the chief broke in. "'Tis not my meaning. But at Rosbrin there was a book written by Fineen the son of Diarmaid, an uncle of my father's father, and my father heard it read from this book that the world turned around one way, like a duck on a spit, and the sun turned around the other way, and that was why they were apart all night. And often I come here, and I swear there is a movement under my feet. But elsewhere there is none, not in the bawn, or in the towers, or anywhere else but just here."

The old man inclined his face, as if he could see the ground he stood upon, but shook his head after a moment's waiting. "It would not be true, Murty," he suggested. "Old Fineen had a mighty scholarship, as I have heard, and he made an end to edify the angels, but—but—"

Murtogh did not wait for the hesitating conclusion. "I saw his tomb when I was a lad, in the chapel at Rosbrin. He was laid at his own desire under a weight of stone like my wall here. I saw even then how foolish it was. These landsmen have no proper sense. How will they rise at the blessed resurrection with all that burden of stone to hold them down? I have a better understanding than that. I buried my father, as he buried his father, out yonder in the sea. And I will be buried there, too, and my son after me—and if I have other children—" he stole a swift glance at the old man's withered face as he spoke—"if I have others, I say, it will be my command that they shall follow me there, when their time comes. I make you witness to that wish, Owny Hea."

The bard hung his head. "As if my time would not come first!" he said, for the mere sake of saying something. Then, gathering courage, he pulled upon the strong arm which was still locked in his and raised his head to speak softly in the O'Mahony's ear.

"If only the desire of your heart were given you, Murty," he murmured; "if only once I could hold the babe of yours to my breast, and put its pretty little hands in my beard—I'd be fit to pray for the men who took my eyes from me. And Murty dear,"—his voice rose in tremulous entreaty as he went on—"tell me, Murty—I'm of an age to be your father's father, and I've no eyesight to shame you—is she—is your holy wife coming to see her duty differently? Have you hope that—that—?"

Murtogh turned abruptly on his heel, swinging his companion round with him. They walked a dozen paces toward the seagate of the castles before he spoke. "You have never seen her, Owny!" he said, gravely. "You do not know at all how beautiful she is. It is not in the power of your mind to imagine it. There is no one like her in all the world. She is not just flesh and blood like you, Owny, or even like me. I am a great Lord among men, Owny, and I am not afraid of any man. I would put the McCarthy, or even the Earl of Desmond, over my cliff like a rat, if he came to me here, and would not do me honor. But whenever I come where she sits, I am like a little dirty boy, frightened before a great shrine of our Blessed Lady, all with jewels and lights and incense. I take shame to myself when she looks at me, that there are such things in my heart for her to see."

Owny sighed deeply. "The grandest princess in the world might be proud to be mated to you, Murty," he urged.

"True enough," responded Murtogh, with candor. "But she is not a princess—or any mere woman at all. She is a saint. Perhaps she is more still. Listen, Owny. Do you remember how I took her—how I swam for her through the breakers—and snapped the bone of my arm to keep the mast of their wreck from crushing her when the wave flung it upon us, and still made land with her head on my neck, and hung to the bare rock against all the devils of the sea sucking to pull me down—?"

"Is it not all in my song?" said Owny, with gentle reproach.

"Owny, man, listen!" said Murtogh, halting and giving new impressiveness to his tone. "I took her from the water. Her companions were gone; their vessel was gone. Did we ever see sign of them afterward? And her family—the Sigersons of that island beyond Tiobrad—when men of mine sailed thither and asked for Hugh, Son of Art, were they not told that the O'Flaherty had passed over the island and left nothing alive on it the size of a mussel shell? Draw nearer to me, Owny. You will be thinking the more without your eyes. Have you thought that it may be she—whisper now!—that she may belong to the water?"

They stood motionless in the gathering twilight, and the bard turned the problem over deliberately. At last he seemed to shake his head. "*They* would not be displaying such piety, as the old stories of them go," he suggested, "or—I mean it well to you, Murty—or breaking husband's hearts with vows of celibacy."

The O'Mahony pushed the old man from him. "Then if she be a saint," he cried, "why then it were better for me to make ten thousand more blind men like you, and tear my own eyes out, and lead you all headlong over the cliff there, than risk the littlest offence to her pure soul!"

The old bard held out a warning hand. "People are coming!" he said. Then, gliding toward his chief, he seized the protecting arm again, and patted it, and fawned against it. "Where you go, Murty," he said eagerly, "I follow. What you say, I say."

Some dancing lights had suddenly revealed themselves at the corner of the nearest castle wall. Murtogh had not realized before that it was dusk. "They will be looking for me," he said, and moved forward, guiding his companion's steps. The thought that with Owny it was always dark rose in him, and drove other things away.

Three men with torches came up—rough men with bare legs and a single skirt-like tunic of yellow woolen cloth, and uncovered heads with tangled and matted shocks of black hair. The lights they boar gleamed again in the fierce eyes which looked out from under their forelocks.

"O'Mahony," one of them said, "the *liathan* priest is at the gate—young Donogh, son of Donogh *Bhade* who fled to Spain. He is called Father Donatus now."

"What will he want here?" growled Murtogh. "I have beaten his father; if I have the mind, his tonsure will not hold me from beating him also."

"He has brought a foreign Spaniard, a young man with breeches and a sword, who comes to you from the King of Spain."

Murtogh straightened himself, and disengaged the arm of the blind man. "Run forward, you two," he ordered sharply, "and call all the men from the bawns and the cattle and the boats, and I will have them light torches, and stand in a line from the second tower to the postern, and show their spears well in front, and be silent. I will not have any man talk but myself, or thrust himself into notice. We were Kings of Rathlin, and we have our own matters to discuss with the Kings of Spain."

II

Three score fighting men, some bearing lights, and all showing shields, and spears, or javelins, or long, hooked axes, crowded in the semblance of a line along the narrow way to the large keep—and behind them packed four times their number of women and children—watched Murtogh when he brought his guests past from the gate.

He moved proudly up the boreen with a slow step and the gleam of a high nature in his eyes. His own people saw afresh how great was his right to be proud. The broad, hard muscles of his legs, straining to burst their twisted leather thongs as he walked; the vast weight and thickness of the breast and shoulders, under the thin summer cloak of cloth from the Low Countries which he held wrapped tight about them; the corded sinews of his big bare neck; above all, the lion-like head, with its dauntless regard and its splendid brown-black mane, and the sparkle of gold in the bushing glibb on his brow—where else in all Ireland would their match be found?[4] But for that strange injunction to silence, the fighters of the sept would be splitting the air with yells for the chieftain. They struck their weapons to-

4. Glibb (Gaelic). Irish manner of brushing one's hair forward over one's brows in a thick mass, perhaps for protection from blows in battle. Spenser notes "Their going to battle without armor on their bodies or heads, but trusting to the thickness of their Glibbs, the which (they say) will sometimes bear off a good stroke." *A View of the Present State of Ireland*, 62.

gether and made the gaze they bent upon him burn with meaning, and he, without looking, read it and bore himself more nobly yet; and the mothers and wives and little ones, huddled behind in the darkness, groaned aloud with the pain of their joy in Murty *Mordha*.

It swelled the greatness of Murtogh when they looked upon those who followed him. "It is the *soggarth liathan*,"[5] they whispered, at view of the young priest, with his pointed face and untimely whitened hair. He would not turn his ferret glance to right or left, as he followed close in his cousin's lordly footsteps, for the reason that these sea-wolves of Dunlogher had ravaged and burnt his father's country within the year, and slain his brother, and gnashed their teeth now, even as he passed, for rage at the sight of him.

And the messenger who came to speak to Murty the words of the King of Spain! They grinned as they stared upon him. An eel-fly, a lame fledgling gull, a young crab that has lost its shell—thus they murmured of him. His legs were scarce the bigness of a Cape woman's arms and were clad in red silken cloth stretched as close as skin.[6] He had foolish little feet, with boots of yellow leather rising to the knee, and from the mid-thigh to the waist were unseemly bulging breeches, blown out like a buoy, and gashed downwise with stripes of glowing colors repeated again in his flowing sleeves. His burnished steel corselet and long reed-like sword would be toys for children in Dunlogher. His face, under its wide-plumed hat of drab felt, was that

5. "Soggarth" means priest. "Liathan" means prematurely white-haired. Father Donatus's white hair may be the result of the shock of Murtogh's sack of the priest's home settlement and the murder of his father, Donogh Bhade, at Ballydevlin a year earlier.

6. The aristocratic Spaniard's physique strikes these people as puny. They are a rugged breed—used to climbing sheer cliffs. Danno O'Mahony, the famous strongman and professional wrestler of the 1930s, for example, was from Ballydehob, not far from the setting of this story.

of no soldier at all—a thin, smooth, rounded face of a strange smoky darkness of hue, with tiny upturned moustachios and delicately bended nose. And the eyes of him! They seemed to be the half of his countenance in size, what with their great dusky-white balls, and sloe black centers, and their thick raven fringes and brows that joined each other. The armed kerns[7] who stood nearest took not much heed of these eyes, but the older women, peeping between their shoulders, saw little else, and they made the sign of the cross at the sight.

When two hours had passed, the baser folk of Dunlogher knew roughly what was in the wind. Two wayfaring men of humble station had come in the train of the Spaniard, and though they had no Irish, their story somehow made itself told. A ship from Spain, which indeed Dunlogher had seen pass a week before, had put in at Dingle, on the Kerry coast, and had landed James Fitzmaurice, the papal legate Sanders, some other clergy, and a score and more Spanish gentlemen or men at arms with a banner blessed by the Holy Father. A great army from Spain and Italy would follow in their wake. But, meantime, the firstcomers were building a fort at Smerwick, and the clan of Fitzgerald was up, and messengers were flying through the length and breadth of Munster and Connaught, passing the word to the Catholic chiefs that the hour of driving the English into the sea was at hand.[8]

The lower floors of the castle and the pleasant grassy bawns outside, cool with the soft sea wind of the summer night, were stirred to a common fervor by these tidings. The other O'Mahonys, the chiefs of Dunmanus and Dunbeekin onto the

7. Warriors.

8. The preparations for what was to be the "Second Desmond Rebellion" are under way here. It is therefore spring/early summer 1579. The Fitzgerald dynasty of Munster, within which the O'Mahonys were a subclan, initiated the uprising supported by Spanish and Italian troops and financially backed by Rome. The rebellion-invasion would end in failure on the coast of Kerry in 1583.

north, of Ballydevlin, Leamcon, Ardintenant, and Rosbrin to the south, and elsewhere in Desmond the O'Sullivan's, MacCarthys, O'Driscolls, and the rest were clashing their shields.[9] Ah, when should they see Murty striding into the field!

In the big hall overhead, where—after three courses of stone stairs were climbed, so narrow that a man in armor must needs walk sideways—the abode of the chieftain and his own blood began, Murtogh was ready to hear the message of the King of Spain.

The broad, rough-hewn table, with its dishes of half-cleaned bones and broken cheeses and bread, it's drinking horns and flagons, and litter of knives and spoons, had been given over to the master's greyhounds, who stood with forepaws on the board and insinuated their long necks and muzzles noiselessly here and there among the remains of the meal. A clump of reeds, immersed in a Brazier of fish oil, burned smokily among the dishes for light.

When, at the finish of the eating, Murtogh had given the signal for departure to the dozen strong men nearest akin to him, or in his best favor, there were left only his son, a slow, good lad born of a first wife long since dead, the blind Owny, the Spaniard, and the *liathan* young priest.

Then Murtogh said to this last man: "Donogh, son of Donogh *Bhade*, I have not frowned on you nor struck you, for the reason that you are my guest. But because my hand is open to you, it is no reason that I should lie and pretend that I am your friend or you mine. Your brother, Diarmaid, the one I could not get to kill, calls himself my heir and twice has sought to take the life of my son here, my Donna *baoth*.[10] Therefore, I will have you go now, and sit below with the others, or read your prayers in your

9. Desmond was an ancient territorial designation in Ireland for a large area of south and southwest Munster.
10. Silly, simple.

chamber where you are to sleep, because I will hear now what the King of Spain says to me, and that is not meant for your ears."

The priest stood on his feet. "Your pride does not become you, Murty *Mordha*," he said, "when I am come to you for your soul's sake and the glory of religion." His voice was thin and high-pitched, but there was no fear in it.

"I will not be taking trouble for my soul just now," replied Murty; "that will be for another time, when I am like to die. And then I will have my own confessor, and not you, nor anyone like you. So you will go now, as I bid you."

Father Donatus, standing still, curled his lips in a hard smile. "You are a great man, Murty! You could dishonor my father and slay my brother like the headstrong bullock that you are, but there are things you cannot do. You cannot lay your finger to me because I come on the business of God."

"It is the business of the King of Spain that I will be thinking of," said Murty with curtness.

"They are the same," rejoined the young priest. "And you are wrong to say what you will be thinking of, because you have not a mind to think at all. If you could think, you would know that you cannot have the words of the King of Spain except when I interpret them to you. This noble gentleman who comes with me speaks more tongues than one, but he has no Irish, and you—it is well known that you have nothing else. Don Tello has sat at your side for two hours, and you have not observed that each word between him and you came and went through me. Oh, yes; you are a great man, Murty, but your mind is not of a high order."

The chieftain rose also. The blood came into his face, and he laid a strong hand on the hilt of his broadsword. But the foot that he lifted he set down again, and he looked at his kinsman, the *liathan* priest, and did not move toward him. "You are in the right to wear a gown," he said slowly, "because you have the tongue and the evil temper of an ugly girl. You speak foolish things in your heat, and they disgrace you. I have the best mind that any man in my family ever had. I have more thoughts in my mind than there are words in your Latin book. I would speak whatever I chose to this gentleman, and I would understand his speech when I troubled myself to do so. But I will not do that—for some time at least; I will have my wife come, and she will sit here, and she will tell me his words, and I will be taking my ease."

Murtogh *Mordha* called his son to his side and gave him a message to deliver.

The priest, smiling in his cold away, leant over and spoke for the space of a minute in a tongue strange to Dunlogher into the Spaniard's ear. Then he stood erect, and gazed at Murtogh with an ill-omened look, and so turned and strode after the lad out of the door.

III

A young woman of the rarest beauty, tall and slender, and with the carriage of a great lady, came into the chamber and moved across to the high, carved chair which Murtogh made ready for her, and seated herself upon it as upon a throne. She had a pale, fair skin, and her hair, coiled heavily in plaits upon her shoulders, was of the hue of a red harvest sun. There were jewels in this hair and upon her throat and hands, and her long robes were of rich, shining stuffs. A chain of wooden beads, with a cross of gold at the end, hung from her girdle, and she gathered this in her fingers as she sat.

The boy, Donogh *baoth*, came with her and crouched in humility on the floor at her side. His thick form and dark hair, and his overlarge head, spoke a likeness now to his father which was not to be noted before. When, as if under the spell of her attraction, he nestled nearer the lady's chair and touched her garment with his hand, she drew it away.

Murtogh *Mordha*, before he took his seat again, and leant back to half lie upon the skins thrown over it, told her the Spaniard's name and explained to her his errand. The Spaniard, bowing himself low, sank upon one knee and reverently kissed her hand, as Murty had seen his father kiss the ring of the Bishop of Ross. He was proud to observe this, because his wife was holier and more saintly still than any bishop.

The lady smiled upon the Spaniard, and all that she said to him, and he to her, was in his tongue. "I cannot speak it well," she said. Her voice had the sweetness of a perfume in the air. "I lived at Seville, in the old convent there, for only two years. I have no joy of remembrance now, save in the peace and charm of those years there, but I fear my memory of the dear speech is dimmed. But I will listen with all my ears—and oh, so gladly!"

She fastened her regard upon his eyes—the great, rolling, midnight eyes—and held it there, that she might the better follow his speech.

"Beautiful lady," the Spaniard said, "I learn only now the power our language, spoken by such lips, may have to enthrall the hearing. Condone my error, I pray you, but I caught from Father Donatus that you were this strong chieftain's wife, and I see that you are his daughter; and even that is strange, to look upon him and *you*."

"I am his wife, but only in name, naught else," she answered. The wave of comprehension sweeping over the surface of the Spaniard's eyes made instant confidence between them. "I am in captivity here. He is a pirate, a Goth, a murderous barbarity. He and his savages here—but of this more a little hence. I beg you now to speak something of your mission—your errand here. He is as helpless to follow our words as one of those hounds; but no dog is keener to suspicion."

The Spaniard, with eager swiftness of speech, piled one upon another the curtailed topics of his business. The lady, moving her fingers along the beads, gleaned the narrow pith of it and dressed it forth in new phrases for the lord of Dunlogher.

"*The King of Spain will send this month,*" she said in the Irish, "*a mighty army to drive the heretic English to the last man from this Island of Saints. They have wounded God too long! The last drop of heaven's patience is dried up by their crimes. Their queen was not born in lawful wedlock, and the Blessed Sacraments are daily profaned by her and her accursed people. Those who sustain and honor God now will be sustained and honored by Him through glorious Eternity.*"

"These things are well known to me," said Murtogh. "I would not need the King of Spain to tell them to me. How will he speak concerning myself?"

The lady was not afraid to smile into the eyes of the Spaniard. "You are to speak after a moment or two," she told him, with a calm voice; "but hear me this little first. My heart is broken here. I do not know how I have had the courage to live. These jewels I wear, the fabrics of my raiment, the wines on the board yonder, are all the booty of bloodstained waves down at the foot to this terrible cliff. He and his savages burn false lights, and lure ships to the rocks, and rob and murder their people. It was thus unhappily I came here, and in fear of my life, while I was still half dead from the water, I suffered the marriage words to be read over me—but now you must speak."

"I would show you tears rather than words, dear lady," the Spaniard said; "and blows on your behalf more preferably than either. Father Donatus whispered the tithe of this to me. The whole truth burns like fire in my heart. As my fathers gave their life blood to drive the infidel from Granada—so I lay my own poor life at your dear feet. If aught but harm to you could come from it, I would slay him now where he lolls there on the skins. He is looking at you now, waiting for you to speak."

"*The King of Spain has heard much of you,*" she began in the

Irish, without turning her head. "*He is filled with admiration for your strength and valor. He desires deeply to know what you will be doing. When you will take arms and join him with your great might in the battles, then there cannot be any doubt of his victory.*"

"That it is easy to see," replied Murtogh. "But the King of Spain's battles are not my battles. There would be some reason to be given, to call me out for his wars. The English will be doing me no hurt. They cannot come here to me, by water or by land; and if they did I would not let any of them depart alive. For what cause should I go to them? Let the King of Spain tell me what it would be in his mind to do on my behalf, when I did the same for him."

The lady spoke to the Spaniard. "The last of my people are killed. They would not have seemed different to you perhaps—to you who are bred in the gentle graces of Spain—but they were not the ferocious barbarians these O'Mahonys are. My father was learned in Latin and English, and it was his dream that I should wed in Spain."

"Oh, rapturous vision!" said Don Tello, with new flames kindling in his eyes. "And if it shall be proved prophetic as well, beautiful lady! Something of this, too, the priest whispered; but the precious words return to me as your dear lips breathed them forth—'wife only in name.' I long to hear them once again."

The lady repeated them, with tender deliberation, and a languorous gleam in her blue eyes began to answer his burning gaze. "I have held the fierce beast at arm's length," she said, "because he is also a fool. I would give a year of my life to be able to laugh in his face and slap these beads across it. I have told him—the blessed thought came to me even while we knelt at the altar together—that I am bound by a vow. His big empty head is open to all the fancies that fly. He believes that an enchanted woman drives up her horses from the bottom of the lake, down at the foot of the small tower here, every night for food; and he spreads corn for them, which the thieves about him fatten on. He believes in witches rising from the sea, and leprechauns, and changelings, like any ignorant herdsman out in the bog, but he is a frightened Churchman, too. He believes that I am a saint!"

"As I swear by the grave of my mother, you are!" panted Don Tello. "But speak now to him."

"*The King of Spain will do very great things on your behalf,*" she recited, in Murtogh's tongue. "*He will make you of the rank of a commander in his armies, and he will ennoble you.*"

"I am noble now," Murtogh made comment, "as noble as the King of Spain himself. I am not a MacCarthy or an O'Driscoll, that I would be craving titles to my name."

"*Then he will send large rich ships here,*" she began again, with weariness in her tone, "*to bring you costly presents. And the Pope, he will grant you ten years' indulgence,—or it may be twenty.*"

"Ask him," broke in Murtogh, sitting up with a brightened face, his hand outstretched to secure silence for the thought that stirred within him—"ask if the Holy Father would be granting just the one spiritual favor I would beg. Will this gentleman bind the King of Spain to that?"

"And may I wholly trust," she asked the Spaniard, with half-closed eyes, through which shone the invitation of her mood, "may I trust your knightly proffer to help? Do not answer till I have finished. You are the first who has come to me—here in this awful dungeon—and I have opened my heart to you as perhaps I should not. But you have the blood of youth in your veins, like me; you are gallant and of high lineage; you are from the land where chivalry is the law of gentle life—is it true that you will be my champion?"

The Spaniard rose with solemn dignity, though his great eyes flashed devouringly upon her, and his breast heaved under its cuirass. He half lifted his sword from the sheath and kissed the cross of its hilt. "Oh my beloved, I swear!" he said, in somber earnestness.

She translated the action and utterance to Murtogh. "*Whatever of a spiritual nature you would crave of his Holiness he would grant.*"

"But it would be a cruel time of waiting, to send all the long way to Rome and back," he objected, "and this matter lies like lead upon my soul."

She looked up into the Spaniard's eyes, and let her own lashes tremble, and fed the ravening conflagration of his gaze with a little sigh. "It would be very sweet to believe," she murmured, "too sweet for sense, I fear me. Nay, Don Tello, I need not such a world of persuasion—only—only—lift your right hand, with thumb and two fingers out, and swear again. And say, 'Bera, I swear!'"

"It is your name?" he asked, and as she closed her eyes in assent, and slowly opened them to behold his oath, he lifted the fingers and waved them toward her, and passionately whispered, "Bera, queen of my heaven, star of my soul, I swear!"

"*That is the sign of the pope himself,*" she explained, with indifference, to Murtogh. "*Whatever wish you offered up you have it already granted. It is Don Tello who bears the holy authority from the pope.*"

The lord of Dunlogher hurled himself to his feet with a boisterous energy before which the lady, wondering, drew herself away. He stretched his bared arms toward her, then flung them upward as in invocation to the skies. The beatitude of some vast triumph illumined his glance.

"Oh, then, indeed, I am Murty *Mordha*!" he cried. "It is I who am prouder than all the kings on earth! It is I who has won my love! Oh, glory to the heavens that send me this joy! Glory and the praise of the saints! Glory! Glory!"

The rhapsody was without meaning to the Spaniard. He

stared in astonishment at the big chieftain with the shining countenance who shouted with such vehemence up at the oaken roof. Turning a glance of inquiry at the lady, he saw that she had grown white-faced and was cowering backward in her chair.

"Our Lady save us!" she gasped at him in Spanish. "He has asked the pope to absolve me from my vow."

Don Tello, no wiser, put his hand to his sword. "Tell me quickly what it is? What am I to do?" he demanded of her.

Murtogh, with a smile from the heart moistening his eyes and transfiguring all his face, strode to the Spaniard, grasped his reluctant hand between his own broad palms, and gripped it with the fervor of a giant.

"I would have you tell him," he called out to the Lady Bera. "Tell him that he has no other friend in any land who will do for him what Murty *Mordha* will be doing. I will ride with him into battle and take all his blows on my back. I will call him my son and my brother. Whatever he will wish, I will give it to him. And all his enemies I will slay and put down for him to walk upon. Oh, Bera, the jewel restored to me, the beautiful gem I saved from the waters, tell him these things for me! Why will your lips be so silent? Would they be waiting for my kisses to waken them? And Donogh, son of mine, come hither and take my other son's hand. I will hear you swear to keep my loyalty to him the same as myself. And Owny Hea—hither, man! You cannot see my benefactor, the man I will be giving my life for, but you have heard his voice. You will not forget it."

The absence of all other sound of a sudden caught Murtogh's ear and checked his flow of joyous words. He looked with bewilderment at the figure of his wife in the chair, motionless with clenched hands on her knees and eyes fixed in a dazed stare upon vacancy. He turned again, and noted that Owny Hea had come up to the Spaniard, and was standing before him so close that their faces were near touching.

The old blind man had the smile of an infant on his withered face. He lifted his left hand to the Spaniard's breast and passed it curiously over the corselet and its throat-plate and arm-holes, muttering in Irish to himself, "I will not forget. I will not at all forget."

A zigzag flash of light darted briefly somewhere across Murtogh's vision. Looking with more intentness, he saw that both of the blind man's hands were at the armpit of the Spaniard, and pulled upon something not visible. Don Tello's big eyes seemed bursting from their black- fringed sockets. His face was distorted, and he curled the fingers of his hand like stiffened talons, and clawed once into the air with them. Then Owny Hea pushed him, and he pitched sprawling against Murtogh's legs, and rolled inert to the floor. His hot blood washed over Murtogh's sandaled feet.

A woman's shriek of horror burst into the air, and the hounds moaned and glided forward. Murtogh did not know why he stood so still. He could not rightly think upon what was happening, or put his mind to it. The bones in his arms were chilled and would not move for him. He gazed with round eyes at Owny and at the red dripping knife which the bard stretched out to him. He felt the rough tongue of a dog on his ankle. The dark corners of the chamber seemed to be moving from him a long distance away. There was a spell upon him, and he could not tremble.

The voice of Owny Hea came to him, and though it was soundless, like the speech of dreamland, he heard all its words: "Murtogh son of Teige, I have slain your guest for the reason that I have the Spanish, and I knew the meaning of his words to this woman, and he could not live any longer. The *liathan* priest, when he would be going, told this stranger that she you called your wife was your enemy, and made a mockery of you, and would give ear gladly to any means of dishonoring you. And the *liathan* priest spoke truly. While the woman repeated lies to you of the King of Spain and the pope, she whispered foul scandal of you, and wicked love-words to that dog's meat at your feet. It is I, Owen, son of Aodh, who tell you these things. And now you know what you have to do!"

Murtogh turned slowly to the lady. She lay, without motion, in her chair, her head limp upon her shoulder, and the whiteness of sea foam on her cheek. Thoughts came again into his brain.

"I have the wisest mind of all in my family," he said; "I know what it is I will be doing."

He drew the short sword from his girdle and put his nail along its edge.

"Donogh *baoth*," he said to his son, "go below and seek out Conogher *tuathal* and Shane *buidhe*, and bid them to seize the *liathan* priest between them, and bring him to me here where I am. And you will take some sleep for yourself then, for it is a late hour."

The lad looked at the pale lady with the closed eyes and at the sword in his father's hand. He set his teeth together and lifted his head.

"I am of years enough to see it all," he said. "I have no sleep on my eyes."

Murtogh bent over the corpse at his feet and caressed the boy's head with his hand. "I will not call you *baoth* (simple) anymore," he said, fondly. "You are my true son, and here is my ring for your finger; you may return with them when they fetch me my *liathan* cousin."

IV

Next morning, young Donogh gave his word to the men of Dunlogher, and they obeyed him, for in the one night he had thrown aside his sluggish boyhood, and they saw his father's ring on his finger, and heard a good authority in his voice. They came out from the western gate at his command, threescore and more, and stood from the brink of the cliff inward, with their weapons in their hands, and made a path between them. But the women and children Donogh bade remain within the bawn, and he shut the inner gate upon them. It was as if the smell of blood came to them there, for the old women put up a lamentation of death, and the others cried aloud, till noise spread to the men on the cliff. They looked one to another and held their silence.

They did not clash their spears together when, after a long waiting, Murtogh came from the gate and walked toward them. A fine rain was in the air, and the skies and sea were grey, and the troubled man would have no spirit for such greeting.

He bore upon his broad back a great shapeless bundle thrice his own bulk. The weight of it bent his body and swayed his footsteps as he came. The cover of it was the skins of wild beasts, sewn rudely with thongs, and through the gaps in this cover some of the men saw stained foreign cloths and the plume of a hat, and some a shoe with a priest's buckle, and some the marble hand of a fair woman. But no word was spoken, and Murtogh, coming to the edge, heaved his huge shoulders upward, and the bundle leaped out of sight.

Then Murtogh turned and looked all his fighting men in their faces, and smiled in gentleness upon them, and they saw that in that same night, while the "little people" had changed Donogh into a man, they had made Murtogh a child again.

"She came up from the water," he said to them, in a voice no man knew. "It was I who brought her out of the water and fought for her with the demons under the rocks, and beat all of them off. But one of them I did not make the sign of the cross before, and that one is the King of Spain; and so he has wrought me this mischief and made all my labor as nothing; and she is in the water again, and I must be going to fetch her out rightly this time."

Murtogh sprang like a deer into the air, with a mighty bound which bore him far over the edge of the cliff. Some there were, in the throng that sprang forward, agile enough to be looking down the abyss before his dissent was finished. These, to their amazement, beheld a miracle. For the great fall did not kill Murtogh *Mordha*, but the waters boiled and rose to meet him, and held him up on their tossing currents as he swam forward, and marked with a pallid breadth of foam his path out to sea, farther and farther out, till the mists hid him from human view.

The wailing song of Owny Hea rose through the wet air above the keening of the women in the bawn. But louder still was the voice of the lad who wore his father's ring, who drew now from beneath his mantle his father's sword.

"I am Donogh, son of Murtogh *Mordha*!" he shouted, "and I am Lord in Dunlogher, and when I am of my full strength I will kill the King of Spain and give his castles and all his lands and herds and women to you for your own!"

The three towers of Dunlogher are broken, and the witch has fled from its grey lake. And no man knows where the bones of its forgotten sept are buried. But the evil currents will never tire of writhing, and the shadows which are no shadows are forever changing, in the Path of Murty the Proud.

Chapter 5

THE WOOING OF TEIGE

c. 1582

The old moon would be seen no more, and the night was very black. The waters swelled, hissing landward, under the cold, hard wind that led in the tide.

Teige, son of Diarmaid *Bhade*, bending forward in his seat in the longboat between the rowers, looked with all his eyes into the inky space about him.[1] The ceaseless plunge and lifting of the boat gave him well enough the measure of the waves they rode. In good time would come the guiding clamor of the breakers tearing at the cliffs which stood as watchtowers to his haven. There was no fear in his thoughts, or in the minds of his men, of harm from the sea that bore them. Yet ever he stared with anxious gaze into the darkness, and now he gasped and put forth his hand.

"You would have seen it *this* time?" he demanded of the man nearest him.

Flann, kneeling in his place, pushed his paddle through the weight of water that held it. Then, as the boat glided downward, he spoke without turning his head.

"What is it a man would be seeing with this blackness on him?"

1. Teige, as a son of Diarmaid, would be a brother to the priest in "The Path of Murtogh." Frederic may have planned to expand upon such relationships in other stories in the long run.

"It is the third time!" answered Teige, in eager tones. "A small burning light at the top of the waves—close here to our side. And I have knowledge now what it signifies. It is a corpse-candle, Flann, that I have seen on the waters! Three times it has been lit for me, and not at all for you—what should be the meaning of that?" He lifted his head and put out a strong voice: "Bend your weight upon the stick, Manus, and you, Tomaltagh, and those before you! There are tidings for us on the land. At the first gate we will be hearing new things!"

But at the first gate there was black silence. Teige and his nine men had brought their boat safely round between the unseen crags, and through the foaming ridge of weed-laden breakers beyond, and dragged it up into the shelter of the higher rocks without a slip of the foot. They had gathered its burden of wreckers' booty into their arms,[2] and, thus laden, had climbed noiselessly along the dizzy path from one narrow foothold to another, up the face of the cliff, with no need for a light. Now, when the sea-wall of Ballydevlin barred their progress, they halted, and Teige blew a loud, braying blast upon the horn slung at his back.

Here, on the height, the shape of things could be dimly distinguished. Above the tall masonry of the gateway and wall, a vague grey difference marked the skyline. Faintly discerning one another, the men murmured complainingly at the delay. Teige, standing foremost, sent echoes rolling from the horn once more and then, with a backward step, slung his axe to strike the door.

"The gate is open!" cried another, of keener vision; and Teige, checking the weapon and its circuit, let it sink upon his shoulder with a doubtful laugh. He pushed forward, and there was nothing to hinder him. The men followed on behind him,

2. O'Mahony clans of the Ivehagh coast, as mentioned in the introduction, frequently salvaged material from shipwrecks. This, as well as piracy, and the charging of harbor dues to foreign vessels, was a major source of income (Rev. J. O'Mahony, *History of the O'Mahony Septs of Kinelmeky and Ivagha*, 109).

under the heavy roof of the gateway and up the grass-grown slope of the outer bawn. The high bulk of the castle pile, uncertain in the blackness, was visible to them. And now, rising above the splashing din of the waters down behind them, their ears caught sounds of another sort—the vibrant ring of harp strings and the chatter of human voices.

"It was my word that tidings would await us," said Teige over his shoulder to Flann.

Of a sudden, a glare of red light close at hand smote his eyes. Blinking and frowning at it, he made out a torch, held in wavering fashion by someone who had opened the second gate.

Teige leaped forward and snatched the torch. Casting his axe aside, he seized the bearer by the neck of his shirt, dragged him to his knees, and twisted his head sidewise in the circle of light. It was Malachy *Caoch*, the one-eyed little herd, who crouched and whimpered under Teige's heavy hand.

"My blind eye is uppermost," he whined. "It may be a great hero who lays his hand on me, and I having no knowledge who he is! It is no sin of mine! It should not be stated against me."

With a gentle push of the arm Teige sent the fellow rolling at his feet.

"Look at me through the eye that has been spared you," he said, with laughter in his voice. "Behold me well and carefully. The drink is thick on your calf's face and on your old woman's tongue, but your eye has its brightness. I will be hearing you tell me who I am."[3]

3. Returning home from wreck-salvaging, and having seen the corpse-fire from out at sea, Teige is pretty sure his father has died and that he has himself come into the chieftainship. Ballydevlin has been demoralized and languishing for four years under the feeble leadership of Teige's father after the settlement was sacked by Murtogh of Dunlogher (this is mentioned in "The Path of Murtogh"). Diarmaid, Teige's father, who has now died, was badly wounded in Murtogh's raid and a brother of Teige killed. Teige's bullying of the herd is to mark his own ascendancy and to establish that a strong new leadership, unlike

The herd had risen to his knees. The single black, twinkling little eye that he turned upward to the big man over him was full of cunning and solicitude.

"You *were* the son of the master when you put forth in your boat three days ago, to take a prey in the wake of the ship from Waterford," he ventured, with caution.

"And what is it that I am now?" Teige demanded, in a loud, confident voice. "I will surely take that eye from your head if you have not the good word for me."

Malachy's long jaw twisted itself slowly in a drunken grimace. His eye sparkled like a gem in the torchlight. "Now," he said, speaking as deliberately as he dared—"at this present time in which you do be listening to me, I crave the boon of you, for I am the first to make it known to you—the first to kneel before you—"

Teige thrust the torch upward to the arm's length and with the groan of joy turned on his heel to the men behind him.

"Hail me!" he cried, and marked a flaming circle in the air above his head. "I am come into my lordship. I am Teige, the Magnanimous Son. I did not raise my hand to my father. It is well known to you, and to all men, that he was no proper lord. His voice was hoarse with endless shouting, but no one heeded him. His castle there before you was sacked and burned by Murty *Mordha*, a mere ignorant bullock; my brothers were given up to be slain, and our ships were driven from the water because of his folly. He behaved falsely to his friends, yet took no profit from his artifices; he gave soft words to his enemies, and they trod upon him. He bestowed rich gifts upon the church—much more than was needful—yet they won him no kindness from the saints or the clergy. He made at last a great pilgrimage and brought back with him only the leprosy. He would not even die in his boat, with the blood of his foes to smooth like oil the

---

that of his weak father, will now prevail. As indicated in "The Path of Murtogh," Teige O'Mahony's great-grandfather and Murtogh's grandfather were brothers.

rough waters about him, but lay mewling in his straw through four harvests, with none but old women to hearken to him. And now he has died the death, and I am well rid of him—yet I will have it said that I never struck him. Though it is a wonderful thing, he did not once feel the weight of my hand. I was before all else a good son. And now I will be a good lord to all my people—according to all their deserts."

The armed men had bowed before Teige and struck their weapons together and raised a shout to him. Still bearing the torch aloft, but now with the axe again in his other hand, he led them forward through the inner gate.

"The burial shall be on the night after tomorrow night," he said to the little herd, who shambled beside him. "He shall at least be given the good fortune of the new moon. Where he has gone such help will not be amiss." Malachy shot up a swift glance from his one eye, and, leering, stepped aside beyond the reach of a blow.

"He is buried already," he replied.

As the young chief said nothing, Malachy raised his voice and flung his arm out in a gesture.

"Hold hither the torch, O'Mahony," he urged. "See the stones we have piled upon him—here to your east. Up with you, Sava! And you, Moree! It is the master who is here!"

Two gloomy figures rose haltingly from the ground at the place to which Malachy pointed. The torchlight flared upon their wrinkled, bare shanks and reddened, unshapely feet; from head to knees they were shrouded in black cloaks, from under which proceeded the monotonous, mumbling lamentations of weary and aged crones. Between these hooded mourners Teige now saw a long, narrow mound of pebbles.

He moved about on the bawn, with the torch held low, till he found a small stone. This he picked up, and, returning, tossed it on the heap.

"It will be written in song of me," he said with gravity to his company, "that at the last I was the best son any man ever had."

"Oh, it is you who will be the great lord, moreover!" cried the herd drawing near, with a new burst of confidence.

"Cause meat and pieces of money to be given to these women," commanded Teige, as he moved away. "Who is it that makes music in the hall, Malachy, my small man?"

"A wandering poet from the O'Sullivan's. He was here at the break of the morning, yesterday. God knows how he learned of our death. These poets have the scent of ravens for the burial."

II

"Sing to me again your poem of the young woman. It is more to my mind than the others."

Thus, two hours further into the night, spoke Teige. His burly form sprawled at its ease in the great chair, over against the fireplace, where, though it was summer still by the calendar, some clouds of turf smoked on the stones. His long reddish hair was thrown back from his brows, and the broad face thus made bear, roughened and crimsoned by weather and sun, wore a look of rude kindliness. He plucked idly at the soft yellow down on his cheeks and chin as he lay back in his seat. He had covered his shoulders with a blue mantle; his sandaled feet rested upon a cushion of Italian velvet, which years before his father had had from the sea.

About the large room, on skins and cloaks spread over straw and rushes on the floor, lay the men who called him lord—in all a score, half weaklings or aged creatures, who drove the herds, or drew the nets, or helped the women in the cornfields and the bawns. On the low table in the center were large flasks and jars of pottery and leather, and even a small barrel of shining wood, cunningly hooped—the motley harvest of many wrecks. Drinking vessels of glass, of horn, of metal, and of shells were strewn here and there on the floor beside the men. Of these latter the meaner sort were fast locked in drunken slumber. The rowers from Teige's boat had their way to bemused dreamland still to make. They were stretched on their bellies, for the most part, with elbows propped, hands folded over the drinking mugs before them, and chins upon these hands. Even when they were lifting the drink to their lips, their eyes were fixed upon Teige in his blue mantle, and upon the stranger in the chimney-corner beyond him.

This newcomer, a man of years, short and lean and dryly dark of aspect, wore the simple half-gown and tunic of the humblest of his class. The garments were worn and faded, and the bands wound round his thin old legs were little better than rags. But there were rings upon his fingers, as they moved among the strings of the harp on his knee, and when he held back his head and fixed his black eyes upon the candles guttering in their sconces on the wall above him, he had the face of a proud man, who might have sung to kings.

"The song of the young woman!" repeated Teige. He half closed his eyes, the more fully to understand the charm of what the bard sang, and swung his head to the rhythm and beat with his thick fingers on his chin.

"It is a noble poem." He spoke again when the minstrel's thin voice was silenced. "And will it be what you imagined in your thoughts, or do you know that there is such a young woman? It is your word that her eyes are like the planets of a harvest night, and that her high bosom is whiter than the gull's wing, and that her walking is to be compared with the tread of the red deer in the Glen. There are no young women like this here in all Ivehagh, nor on the islands, nor have I heard reports of such in O'Donovan's country beyond. My brother bore his spears through that land, and he brought on his return no high opinion at all of the women. And if what you sing of is what is in your mind, and nowhere else, I will have you tell me so."

The wandering man stroked the bar of his harp with his ringed fingers and smiled wisely into the eyes of Teige. "It is not I who will be heard singing of Ivehagh," he said, "or of yon paltry islands, much less of the O'Donovan's land of misery and swinish violence. In all these darkened parts there is no man but you that I have seen worthy to listen to a poem of politeness and high feeling. And therefore how will their women be better than themselves? But you are born out of your place here, in these poor surroundings."

Teige's wide brow narrowed itself in frowning lines, and he lifted his head. The bard put out a hand to restrain him, and mixed oil with his voice.

"It is no belittling of you to speak thus," he urged. "The fame of Ballydevlin is very well known to me, as a castle which has needed only such a head as the saints have given it now, to force itself upon the fears of princes and loom darkly in the dreams of kings. And I bless the exceeding good fortune which bent my steps hither—"

"But it is of the young woman that I would be hearing," broke in the chief, with sharpness. "I know my own work very well and do not need to be told by my guests. But about her merits, the warmth of your words stirs my mind, and I have to ask you if she is alive, and has a name in a country, or have you eaten up my time with visions out of your own head?"

The bard sighed softly, even while he stole glances at Teige's huge arms and shoulders, and the weapon at his belt, and the fighting men on the floor in the shadows behind it.

"How should I dare to sing any false thing at your fireside?" he replied. "It would work a great wrong to your hospitality, and I am a humble man whose life is spent in the exercise of gratitude. The subject of my poor poem, though it lifts itself in my esteem since it has your praise—is a short-veiled woman of my own people. It is Grace O'Sullivan that I sing of—the unequaled daughter of a kinsman of mine, the matchless jewel of a family whose women shine in Tiobrad like gems upon a monarch's crown.[4] And what I sang was but a partial rumor, a faint, distant little echo, of the wonderful truth. But you will have been hearing often of the women of the O'Sullivan. Our very name, 'eye of the Sun,' gleams radiantly from the sweet faces of our mothers and sisters, and—"

"But this young woman," interrupted Teige,—"what will be the name of her father, and his country?"

"He is styled Hugh O'Sullivan, of Inverdurrus. His castle is seen from the sea, a lofty fortress under the shadow of a black mountain, beside the leap of a grey stream. It is of these falling waters that I sang—

> When the sun his rounded bow of colors
> Bends against the foaming sheet of mist
> In thy glance a purer radiance—

and the rest."

The bard had picked some chords upon his harp, and made offer to sing the lines once again, but Teige held up a hand to stop him.

"And this Hugh," he pursued the theme, "is he a chieftain of much valor and power? Would he have the victory over me, if we met with our forces in combat?"

The bard smiled doubtfully. "I would give no man the victory over you," he made answer, with caution; "without doubt you would exceed Hugh in a slight measure, but he is a great and redoubtable chieftain, the terror of Tiobrad."

Teige gazed attentively at the little man in silence for a time. "Your judgment has no large value," he said at last. "We are the people of the Coast of White Foam; we are born on the sea, and we wage war from our boats. You O'Sullivans are not of the water, and you would have no comprehension of such matters."

4. Tiobrad = Tipperary.

The stranger lifted his head and wagged it. "There is no kins-man of mine who is not more at home on the waves than in his own bed."

"But you yourself," said Teige: "it is my meaning that you would not be a sea-going man."

"These are my years of decay and calm," replied the other, "and I pass them best on land. But when the fire of youth was in me I loved the water like a fish. With my two hands—before they bore these rings which hospitable lords bestow upon me now for my small skill in entertainment—I have brought a boat of eight from Inverdurrus, past whirlpool and sunken crag, through tempest and high-rushing waves, to within sight of this headland which owns you for its lord."

"This is very good news for me," remarked Teige. He rose on the word to his feet, with the resolute upward spring of a strong man intent upon deeds. At his gesture, and the look on his face, the waking men leaped from the floor and crowded forward.

"To you, Flann, and you, Manus," Teige ordained, "I give you charge of this guest of mine. You are to keep drink from your lips and sleep from your eyelids till the hour after the dawn. He is not to be denied sleep if he will take it, but you will not suffer him to stir beyond the inner gate. And at that hour I will be roused, and with me every man in Ballydevlin, for there is a great feat which I will perform."

The bard of the O'Sullivans had risen as well. The harp trem-bled in his hand, and his small old knees shook together. "I cling to the skirt of your hospitality, O'Mahony!" his alarmed voice quavered.

Teige smiled with broad graciousness upon him. "You are wrapped warmly in the robe of my welcome," he reassured him. "No single grey hair of yours shall be stroked awry. I will be hav-ing you bear me company, as if you were the most favored of my own men. The service you shall render me is very great. I am a young man, and I am in the first hours of my lordship. The drunken people from my father's burial are not yet awake, but I will not sleep in a naked bed until I have announced myself to other princes and chieftains by an achievement worthy of my high spirit."

"But age is heavy on me," pleaded the stranger, with perplexed eyes. "It is a burden and an encumbrance that I would be, in any warlike adventure. My legs are weak underneath me; I cannot move along with strong men in the marching."

"You shall be taking your ease, seated on soft skins in my big vessel," replied Teige calmly. "No task shall be laid upon you, or aught required of you save your counsel. The man who has brought a boat of eight from Inverdurrus hither in his youth can bring a boat of twelve hands to Inverdurrus in the seed time of his life. He will be having it all in his mind."

The O'Sullivan man gazed hard about him, and bit his lip, seeking for words. "But is such great haste becoming to you?" he ventured at last to ask.

"I cannot tarry," said Teige with decision. "In two day's more I should be having the new moon upon my back, and that would be evil fortune for me—and without doubt for you also."

III

"It is indeed a higher mountain than any in my country, or within the site of our people. You have not deceived me at least upon this matter."

Teige, leaning upon his axe, stood upright in the prow of his large boat. The stranger of the O'Sullivans, crouched upon the skins at his feet, seemed shrunken and smaller for the voyage of two days. He held his head above the side of the vessel and stared before him with glassy eyes.

The mountain of Iovar rose grimly from the dark water, black and straight, three arrow- flights away. At its base, on the farther side, a spur of green-clad land spread itself outward to the sea and hung above the breakers' line of foam. The vessel had entered upon calm water; all about it, save at the entrance of its wake, tall cliffs reared themselves, the homes of countless sea-fowl whose screams and flutterings filled the air. It was the hour before the setting of the sun.

"But I do not see the lofty fortress of your kinsman Hugh," pursued Teige. "And the leap of the gray stream—the 'foaming sheet of mist' that your poem celebrated—it is nowhere visible to me."

The large sail had been suffered to drop from the mast. Some of the men held their paddles already in the water and looked inquiringly to their chief.

"It will be very bad for you," Teige said, speaking downward over his shoulder to the little man bent upon the skins, "to be unable to find your kinsman's castle, even now while your eyesight remains to you, because when I shall have lifted the eyes out of your head, then it is still less likely that you will ever be able to come upon it in your wanderings."

The bard gave a shivering groan. "We are close upon it," he murmured hoarsely. "Bid the rowers push across to the north. It is on the other side."

Obedient to the signal, the vessel veered and crept slowly across the gloomy face of Iovar. The low-lying greenland waxed in size as the invaders began to round it. Then it's slope unfolded to their vision—a shepherd's field inset upon the crags, stretching gently forward to the strand. A narrow vertical riband of moisture on the black rocks behind caught the glimmer of the sinking sun.

"In the great heat and dryness the stream has failed," sighed the bard, in a low, husky voice.

Teige, gazing intently upon the prospect, saw now on the upper part of the slope, built in part against the rocks, a kind of small house, piled loosely of stones without any binding of lime. It was of the height of two floors, and its walls showed only slits of an arm's breath instead of windows.

"And will that be the castle—the stronghold of the great and redoubtable chieftain, the terror of Tiobrad?" demanded Teige, with a curling lip. "Is it my eyes that are in fault?—for they reveal to me merely a shepherd's hut. I will be just to you; I will ask my men what it is they behold."

The man of the O'Sullivans bent his head and struck it despairingly upon the boat's side. Then, upon a thought, he lifted it.

"Oh woe! woe!" he moaned. "The fierce O'Moriartys will have been at their bloody work again. In my father's father's time 'tis known that they descended upon us and wrought great havoc in all this country. And now it is plain they have come once more, and put Inverdurrus to the sack, and leveled the noble fortress, and without doubt slain many of the people of my blood. Oh then, the valiant Hugh, the courageous and magnanimous chieftain, is he indeed no more? And Grace, the light of our eyes, the blossom of the beautiful spring upon our ancient stem, is she also gone from us? Oh, heaven's blight on those false savages, the O'Moriartys! May the forked lightning of the black sky descend on them! May the saints' loathliest murrain devour them!"

He had raised his thin voice high in sudden imprecation and made it shake with the fervor of his wrath; but now, at the wave of Teige's hand and a glance into his face, silence fell upon him. He dropped back on the skins and groveled among them.

"Even the O'Moriarty is not without mercy in his bosom," said Teige, with tightened lines about his mouth. "He has left someone alive upon the rock."

The figure of an old man, meanly clad but erect, could be seen moving down the slope to the strand. He halted at a little distance from the water and shaded his eyes with his hand against the glare of the western sky.

The rowers pushed forward, watching him curiously. The

boat's bottom crushed its way over the reeds of the shallows and then rested upon the sands underneath.

"Farther to the north there is an open channel," called the old man. "You cannot come to dry land here."

"It is the great chieftain, Hugh O'Sullivan of Inverdurrus, that I do be seeking," cried Teige, "and if I can come to the sight of him, it is not water to the armpit that will keep us apart."

"I am of that name," shouted back the other; "but I am no chieftain, but simply a small man of the fishing and sundry sheep. It will not be worth any armed man's while to wet himself for me, much less the commander of a host. You are very welcome to come dry, and to please yourself with all I have."

The men with the paddles had pulled the boat off, and now by the old man's guiding hand they made another course and came up to the side of a large stone.

Teige, lifting his foot over the prostrate, huddled form of the bard, leaped onto the land. Then, turning, he stooped and seized the crouching minstrel by the collar of his shirt, and by the force of his arm lifted him out of the boat. The little man, choking and abashed, hung his head upon his breast.

"You are kindly welcome," the shepherd of Inverdurrus repeated, with a courteous inclination, drawing nearer.

Teige looked upon him with surprise. Although his garments were those of a slave, he bore himself with dignity.

"I am greatly beholden to you," Teige made answer. "If it is not a rudeness in me, you have a speech and a behavior which do not fit your place."

"It is the place of my own choosing," Hugh replied, "and I have pleasure in it. No lord molests me here, and I am a free man to live my life. I am so lacking in manly qualities that bloodshed is hateful to me. It was my mischance to be born without the desire to put my foot on any man's neck, or to drive his cattle away, or to make him suffer in any fashion. Yet a stubbornness was in

my blood, so that I could not delight in calling another my master, and cringing to him and doing his bidding, whether he were
prince in his fortress or abbot in his cloister. These are the mis-
fortunes of my character. They bring me to what you behold. Yet
I am not without food to offer you and your people, both white
meats and flesh, and with all strong drink to uphold the stomach. Spanish wines I have none, for I am so strange and outland-
ish a person that I procure no ships to be wrecked on my rocks.
And so I crave that you and your company will follow me."

Teige pulled at his soft beard in meditation. "I have with me
a kinsman of yours," he said thoughtfully. "It was in my mind
that he had done me a mischief, but now my thoughts turn a
little toward another opinion."

The bard shamefacedly lifted his head. His hands he hid under the folds of his short cloak.

"I know him and his rings of base metal very well," remarked
Hugh, gravely surveying the minstrel. "It is Tiarnan *Bladair* (the
flatterer) that you have in your train. He also is welcome here.
His falsehoods and his vanities do not win him friendships as
he grows in years, but they are in his nature, and I am not his
judge. If he has wrought you evil, I as his kinsman will intercede
for him. It will not be for the first time."

Teige's eye roved over the thin trickling line of ooze upon
the cliff in the distance, and the poor house reared against the
rocks. His ruddy big face flushed a deeper red under the impulse of some thought which tugged upon his tongue. From the
land his gaze wandered to the sky, and he stared at what he saw.

"You have a daughter?" he asked suddenly, with abrupt boldness.

The venerable man looked at him, and at the boat behind
him, in turn. Then he bent a prolonged, searching gaze upon
the averted face of his loose-tongued kinsman.

"How is it possible that I should deny it?" he made answer
finally.

"You could not in politeness ask of me my name, but I will offer it to you. I am Teige, son of Diarmaid, son of Conogher *Fionn*, of the People of the Bridge, and in my own right lord of Ballydevlin. And if you speak the harsh word, I will go peacefully now to my boat, and take my men, and return to my own place, and come near you no more. But if you have another word for me, I will stay, and I will ask you now for the gift of your daughter in marriage."

The father observed his guests narrowly, with doubt in his glance. "You have not seen the colleen," he said. "You know of her only by the report of Tiarnan here,—and he is not to be believed in by any prudent man."

"Beyond doubt he is a strong liar," Teige admitted, and they both looked at the bard. "Yet I have my own belief in this matter," the young man went on. "I know that it is good for me to wish for your daughter."

As he spoke he pointed upward to the pale, vague, fleecy crescent in the ashen sky, above the glow of sunset. "When my eyes came upon that new moon, and I beholding it face-to-face, there was nothing in my mind but thoughts upon your daughter. It is plain enough, then, that I must ask for her, and desire her above all things."

"You have the thoughts of a young man," said the father, still gravely regarding him. "Yet it may be that it is as well to be ruled by a woman as by a moon. Perhaps, indeed, it is the same thing. For Grania governs me,[5] and draws me wither she will, even as the tide is led forward, and held, and sent away. But if I would not be choosing to part with my daughter? It would be very black and empty for me here, alone with the sheep and the shellfish and the gulls. And, moreover, if when she beheld you she laughed in your face? I cannot tell what a girl's thoughts would be, to look at you."

5. Grania is a major figure in Irish mythology. See Lady Gregory's play *Grania* and Yeats's *Diarmuid and Grania*.

Teige pulled upon his beard, and smiled ruefully, and glanced upward into the sky again for courage. "I came to do battle for your daughter," he said slowly, "and kill you if you would be standing too stiffly in my way, and lay waste your territory, and bear a bride to my own place with the pride and renown of triumph at arms. But now it is to be seen that I have come upon a fool's quest, and this would make a mock of me, and a mark for the derision of old women and simpletons, if you did not be speaking the wisdom of age to me, and showing me the courtesy of a high station. And this gives me a warm heart toward you, and I look upon you with the tears of the son's fondness in my eyes. And if it is pleasing to you, you shall take the place of my father, and you shall come with me, and sit in the seat of honor at my feasts, and all my people will be bowing low to you when you do be passing. And now will it be your word that I am to depart?"

"I have not bidden you to go," replied the old man, with the dawnings of a smile in his beard. He gave his hand to Teige, and the two turned and moved toward the house of the rock.

The rowers began leaping from the boat, and Tiarnan, his head once more well in air, marshaled them to follow him. As they came up the slope, the form of a young woman, standing at the hurdles, met their eyes. They observed Teige advance toward her, and humble himself in salutation, and then, rising, lift his arm and point to the sky. The girl raised her face to the heavens, and smiled with the blush of a rose at what she beheld and heard, and they saw that she was very beautiful. She took the glance from her father, and gave her hand to Teige.

"The grey stream from the mountains is somehow dried at its spring," said Tiarnan boldly to Flann, "and doubtless through misfortune the great castle I sang of has disappeared. Yet it is plain to me nonetheless that I shall live to wear a gold chain around my neck."

Chapter 6

THE TRUCE OF THE BISHOP

I

A pallid and starved sunlight looked upon the shore-land, and mocked it, because, now, in the fall of the harvest, there was no yield of any kind for the blade, or any reaper to seek it. On all the fair plowlands of the lords of Dunbeekin, stretching along the smooth valley of the bay, and pushing inward over gently lifting slopes to the furze-lined granite barrier of Gabriel, no ditch stood unbroken: the fields lay naked and blackened by fire.[1] The tall keep watched the deserted water with sightless eyes, through which the daylight shone from wall across to wall, and at its feet the crouching huts of its people were thatchless. It was the desolation of conquest. The conquered were dead or in hiding among the hills. The spoilers, their havoc wrought, had turned and gone away, with famine spreading wave-like at their heels.

Far up on the flank of the mountain there fell the distant lowing boom of a bittern.[2] Some cattle, lost in the waste of

1. In this concluding chapter, it is circa 1603, and Turlogh, the young chieftain of Dunbeekin in "In the Shadow of Gabriel," is old and his lands have suffered the onslaught of the Elizabethan armies. His and his people's days are now numbered.

2. "Booming" may seem an odd description of a bird's call, but the deep mating call of this furtive, wetland bird has traditionally been so described—

thicket at a further height, answered this call as if it came from their kind.

Three men, sprawled on their bellies in a grassy crevice between the boulders, had been peering downward upon the picture of ruin below. They glanced at one another now, with a flash of comprehension. A little wiser than their kine, they knew that the bittern cried only in the breeding springtime, and this was the tenth month of the year. One of them echoed the sound, and when it was repeated, coming nearer, the three dragged themselves to their feet, and, stealing upward, stood forth on a ledge of rock in plain view. There climbed toward them presently another, a lean and agile man, whose bare legs brushed through the spikes of furze and heather as if they were cased in hide, and whose naked soles missed no footing on the stones as he bounded from boulder to crag.

He stood panting before them, and without speech turned to survey the prospect spread beneath, till his breath could be overtaken. Looking thus, his rover eye caught something the others had already seen—a small barque, with full sails limply hanging on the still air, down in the misty distance where the great sea ends and Dunmanus begins.[3] He pointed to it, and nodded his head.

"It is to Turlogh, son of the Fineen, I will be hastening now," he said, with abruptness. "Show me the way."

---

as far back as Chaucer's "The Wife of Bath's Tale" (Prologue 978). Sir Thomas Browne, W. G. Sebald notes, is said to have long kept a bittern in his study "in order to find out how this peculiar bird could produce from the depths of its throat such a strange bassoon-like sound, unique in the whole of nature" (*The Rings of Saturn* [New York: New Directions, 1998], 22). An imitation of the bird's call is employed by the messenger and Turlogh's men here as a signal. The bittern became extinct in Ireland in the nineteenth century, but two were cited in Wexford fairly recently—see *IrishTimes.com*, November 13, 2011.

3. The watch is looking far south of Dunbeekin, which is at the northern reach of the bay, well north of where the strange boat would enter Dunmanus Bay from the open sea.

As the group turned, the foremost of them lifted his head and halted.

"It is Turlogh who comes to you," he said

A few paces away, on the crown of the cliff, stood a man to whom all four bent their heads. He regarded them with an eye which asked them questions, yet shrank from hearing these if they were to be not to his mind; and they, knowing this well, held their peace, and looked about them at their ease.

The lord of Dunbeekin was an old man now, tall and slender of frame, with much gray hair flowing upon his rounded shoulders. His apparel of quilted jacket and cloak and tunic, falling to the mid thigh, were of fine cloth but stained and torn by exposure in these rude times that had befallen him. The face he bent upon his tribesmen was long and thin, and marked with many lines. They were skilled from years of use to see in this wrinkled countenance sometimes the cunning of a fox, sometimes the wistful inquiry of a puzzled child; and they never feared him, and would always die for him, and understood when they heard men call him Turlogh of the Two Minds.

"I heard the bull of the bog," he said, giving the bittern its old name among the people. "It was good to the ears." His voice was grave and lingering.

Goron the messenger nodded again. He saw that Turlogh had noted the strange craft entering the bay, and waited for a little more to be questioned. Then he motioned to the others to leave him alone with his chief, and as they moved away he clambered up on the rock.

"O'Mahony, there will be no help coming at all," he said. "Young Donogh, son of Murtogh, will not stir from Dunlogher, for the reason that he is watching the O'Driscolls of the island, to take a prey of cattle from them at the change of the moon. The strong houses of Dunmanus and Ballydevlin and Leamcon are like Dunbeekin there, with the sunlight shining through their windows, and their people are dispersed and have no foot-ing in their country."

"And Conogher of the Cross, in Ardintenant, the head of our sept, the venerable and holy man?" asked Turlogh, with a bitter little jest in his tone. "And Teige of Rosbrin, whom I saved from the MacCarthy, and from his own brother?"

Goron shook his head.

"The English lie between you and them. And they will not be lifting their short fingers for us."

"They will be making peace with the English?" the chief de-manded.

"They will be keeping their tongues behind their teeth," said the other briefly.

It was Turlogh's turn to nod comprehension.

"So it will be the end, then!" he said, musing aloud. "We have been true to God, and He will not restrain the hand of our her-etic enemies. I have been all my days loyal to my family; I have withheld nothing in their service; I have made my Dunbeekin a tower of refuge for all my kinsmen when troubles assailed them, and when their own fathers and brothers sought their lives— and now you do be seeing their gratitude. You have it from me, Goron, son of Tiarnan, there is not in heaven nor on earth any thankfulness for good deeds rendered."

Goron looked into his lord's sad old face and smiled. In stat-ure and girth he might have been Turlogh's twin, but his gar-ments were of the coarsest, and his skin was burned and tanned by the life of a low-born man. His face, lean and pointed like the other's, was shrewd and bluntly single-minded. He stood well enough with his chief, these many years, to speak in freedom.

"I know only what I am told about heaven," he replied, "but the earth I observe with my own eyes. Men will get nothing here but what they can take with their right arm. You have made no one afraid of you, Turlogh, son of Fineen. You have belonged to no man's party, and marched with him to spoil and waste all others. You speak the truth that your cousins found refuge in Dunbeekin from the wrath of their fathers. But it was true as well that these fathers would be coming next year to be protected from the fury of their sons. Your walls were a strong shelter for them both in their day of need, but they left when it was safe to do so without thanks to you in their hearts. They have their own troubles now to weigh them down, but if they had not—then all the same you would not be seeing the color of their blood. And, moreover—there are the books."

The old chief laughed—a mirthless and melancholy laugh.

"They have the right of it," he said, sighing. "They speak the true word—my father should have made a monk of me. I am not a fit master of my people. I have never desolated any man's country, or put out his eyes, or held him sleepless for a single night with terror of me. That is very bad for me. My cousins have only contempt for one who reads in books, and does not be riding out to sack some neighbor's castle, and drive his herds away. Their bards do well to make verses about my bloodless hands." He held out these hands, still unwithered by years, and white and shapely, and viewed them with a gloomy smile. "If they were stained red, my kinsmen would know me for a true O'Mahony— a true son of the People of the Bridge. What will you be thinking, Goron? It will be too late for me to begin now?"

Goron's eyes sparkled.

"If my counsel is asked," he said, promptly, "your people would leap for joy to have one good fight before they die."

Turlogh's face clouded with doubt.

"Poor souls. What would they be doing in a battle? I have made them a mock and a byword in Carbery, Goron. I have taught them to till the land, and take fish from the sea, and make nets and build ditches; and these things they do very well. And if there were some of a war-like nature, with weapons to guard the bawns, all these my brother Donal has drawn with him to the army of the Earl. You yourself were of those who advised to quit Dunbeekin before the English came in sight, and bring hither the women and children and cattle into a place of safety. You spoke no word of resistance when we lay here that night, and looked down, and saw the thatches flame up like torches, and the fire roll through the fields of corn. It was not in your mind to fight then. We saw the black forms of these English against the furnace they made of our corn and our roofs, and we were glad to be at this distance. And why should we be talking otherwise now?"

If his companion had some answer ready, Turlogh did not wait for it. A lifting breath of air had filled the sails of the strange vessel and brought it along up the bay until now it hung in view close to the opposite shore of Muinteravoira. The sight raised new thoughts in the chief's mind.

"Will that be English, too?" He wondered, aloud.

Goron had forgotten this part of his tidings.

"It is a ship from some unknown land," he explained. "I hailed it from the rocks beyond Dunlogher at daybreak. It is a sort of holy miracle, O'Mahony. Our Lord Bishop is in that ship, coming all the way from his pilgrimage to the True Cross. Two years gone he is, and we not knowing if he was alive, and he returning to us now with grand relics and a train of priests. 'Twas with one of them I spoke—a young man walking the deck and reading his prayers. I cried to the blackamoor at the helm to beware the sunken rocks at the headland and waved my arms to force my meaning on him, but the priest had the Irish and called out to me that it was God's ship, with a bishop in it, and holy relics beside, and no harm could come to it or them. But he told the helmsman, nonetheless, the ship's course was laid off."

Turlogh stared at him.

"Is it your meaning that *our* bishop, Lawrence Malmoon

(Luirint Maol-Mughain), son of Ivar, will be in that ship?" he demanded.

"No other," answered Goron.

"But what land will he be making?" pursued the chief, knitting his brows in perplexity as he watched the craft drifting inland. "There is no foothold for him in all Muinteravoira."

"'Tis not Muinteravoira, or any land of the Dalys or Sullivans, he will be touching. His lordship will be coming to you. The priest gave me that word."

The lord of Dunbeekin bent a stern, searching gaze upon his man.

"I will not think you have a trap laid for me, Goron *shuileach*," he said, gravely.

"You will not think it, O'Mahony," responded the other, with proud candor. "It would put too much shame upon you, and upon me also, to think that evil thought."

"I will ask your forgiveness," said Turlogh, hastily. "There is no sleep for me, here in the rocks, and I am very tired. Come with me now, to the place where my people are gathered."

The pale sunlight had lost itself before this in the veil of misty haze drawn over the sky above the line of the distant western peaks. The mountainside lay in the shadowless, tranquil approaches of twilight; silent for a long time, save that from point to point, along its vast terraced expanse of cliffs and moorland, there rose at intervals the trumpeting of an ox-horn—flat yet sonorous. Sounds of rustling through the heather and scrub-furze began to make themselves heard. Then came louder and more confident noises, the shouting of men above the rest.

The first stars, twinkling forth through the smoky residue of sunset, saw a long cavalcade descending by a tortuous broken path the rough face of Gabriel. They came on down through the growing darkness—bareheaded men, wild-faced and savage of attire, leading horses laden with household goods; boys and youths of unkempt, barbarous aspect, herding droves of swift-footed little black cattle along the narrow defiles; tall women, wholly muffled from view in huge hooded cloaks of black and scarlet, bearing burdens upon their heads and dragging forward children by the hands; then more horses and cattle, moving under high bundles of mountain grass and bracken freshly cut; and, at the tail, a score or more of straggling men, with quilted jackets and pikes upon their shoulders.

In front of all walked Turlogh, with his doctor and his chaplain at his side. The last vague glimmer of daylight in the evening air fell upon these three as they felt the burnt stubble of the nearest field under their sandaled feet and saw the black bulk of Dunbeekin loom close before them. There was doubt on the faces of the priest and the leech, but old Turlogh threw his head back and looked into the dusky finish of the day with a smile at his lips and a resolute eye.

II

Hours later, in the shine of the harvest moon, the lord of Dunbeekin stood upon the strand with a moiety of his people and saw others of his men wading waist-deep in the whitened waters bear toward him in their arms his great guest, the bishop.

Already there had come to land, by means of the little boat, some dozen priests and servants. These latter, subtle-faced and proud like all menials of the tonsured folk, held aloof in silence. Two of the younger priests, with the tails of their drenched gowns under their arms, stood at Turlogh's side and spoke to him in whispers of strange matters. The bishop, they said, was in the grasp of a mortal sickness. Nothing but the holy relics he brought with him from Syria had availed to serve his iron will and keep him alive to touch Irish land under his feet once more. These priests had learned something in Spain, and more here along their native coast in the past day, of the grievous burden of woe and spoliation which had been laid upon Munster. They gathered new knowledge now from Turlogh's saddened answers to their queries. All things westward from Cork had been put to the torch and sword. The English had passed over the land like a pestilence. The shadow they cast was death. Where were the English now? Ah, who should say? Somewhere across the hills. No one from Dunbeekin had followed them. It was not credible that they should return to the desert they had made.

"We moved away to the mountainside," explained Turlogh. "They plundered and burned what we left behind. They are distant many miles now, and we have come to our own place again, to welcome our lord bishop. It is a sad thing that he would not be visiting me in the days of my strength and well-being. Now, when at last he comes, we are in ruins, and scarcely the poorest honors can be paid him. No man of our race was a bishop before him. Here in Dunbeekin we would have lighted his path with fires and drained the sea for an offering of its treasures to him. But he would never come to me. He turned always instead to my cousin Conogher, the great man in the White Castle, the head of our tribe, the chief of the pilgrimage. We took grief to us because of that. And here now, at the end, he comes to my gate, and I am in a hard plight and cannot receive him according to his high merits, and he, you say, is sick unto death. I crave of his charity that he will think no evil of our poverty and belittled powers." The chief gave a rueful little laugh. "For the matter of that," he added, "we have each had our day. We are both poor men together. If my castle has been broken, his abbey has no two stones resting one upon another. He does well to come to me. We stood a long league apart in our good days. We can sleep back to belly now, under the common cloak of calamity. They would hang us together, on one limb of a tree, those heretic English wolves."

The more forward of the two priests held up a finger. "He

knows nothing of it at all," he murmured. "We have held it from him. No man of us dared to utter the smallest word of it to him. It is you who must tell him. You are his kinsman, and he will take it from you. He is a cold man with his priests, but he is warm to his own blood."

Turlogh laughed, then starred with round eyes at the speaker, and laughed again.

"He has no knowledge of it at all, you say?"

"Since we set sail with the Genoese captain in Rogation week, from Cyprus, he has heard no word about Ireland.[4] He has too proud a stomach for bad tidings, and no other came to us at any halting place."

Four men, dripping out of the salt water, stood before Turlogh now, or he would have spoken further. They bent and drew short breaths under the stress of what they bore in their arms— a swollen, black-swathed bulk, shapeless as a sack of corn. Turlogh gazed at it in the deep shadows thrown by the men on the moon-side, and was in doubt. Then outlines shaped themselves, and he saw the gross, unwieldy figure of a short man grown unduly fat, with cowled head tipped forward to hide the face. In its hands this shrouded form held a small casket, laid with gold and precious stones. The faint glimmer of these in the moonlight led his eye to a blaze, as of a planet in the obscurity, emitted by a jewel at the side of the box.

The lord of Dunbeekin crossed himself, and, kneeling on the wet sand, kissed the ring of his bishop.

Slowly, as he rose to his feet, the sunken head was lifted, and he saw in the frame of the hood a mask of pallid, lifeless flesh, bloated beyond human semblance. He shuddered as he gazed, and found two strenuous eyes peering into his out of this monstrous visage.

4. Rogation week in the liturgical calendar was the week in which Thursday was the Feast of the Ascension.

"Such as my poor Dunbeekin is, my lord," he said, wonderingly, "it puts itself with pride under your feet."

"Its name shall be exalted above all others," said the bishop. The voice came steady and clear-toned, as if informed by a spirit which carnal decay could not shake. "It is privileged to hold for a night the most priceless and inestimable of earth's treasures— the piece of the True Cross which I bear in my unworthy hands." He pushed the casket forward into the moonlight.

Turlogh knelt again, and with him every man on the strand.

The priests and the bishop's train gave the signal for rising. They looked up toward the keep, where passing lights in the windows bespoke a flutter of preparation. They yawned and moved their feet, like weary men impatient for food and sleep. Turlogh placed himself by the side of the litter-men, still bearing the bishop in their arms, and with them led the way.

"Some small affliction of the blood," said the bishop, as he was borne along up the path, "distorts and enfeebles my members for the moment. When I have placed this holy relic fittingly upon my high altar in Rosscarbery,[5] and given orders for a shrine for it to my chief builders and artificers, I will make a penitential journey to St. Declan's, in sainted Ardmore, and drink from his well, and with his blessed intercession I shall come forth cleansed and whole."[6]

Turlogh looked sidewise across his guest to the faces of the priests behind. Their glances answered his with significance.

"A fire has wrought some mischief in my house," he replied, haltingly; "I fear it is not all repaired as yet. It is the dry season of the year, and the flames had their will. But I will be hoping

5. Rosscarbery, east along the coast from the Ivehagh Peninsula, was historically the ecclesiastical and cultural center of West Carbery and the location of a monastery and a cathedral.

6. St. Declan is one of the most revered Irish saints. Some legends date his mission as pre-Patrician or have him a contemporary of Patrick. His shrine is in Ardmore in Wexford.

and praying that things are not so bad with me that your lordship will be put to discomfort. And after the long voyage in the
ship, will you not be resting here two days, or three? We are
kinsman, my lord, and have grown to gray hairs without coming upon each other till this night, which I account the chief
hour of my life. And I will implore you to stay longer with me,
Lawrence, son of Ivar."

"At a future time, Turlogh, son of Fineen," returned the other.
"But I will be pressing forward tomorrow, with no delay. I have
been two years away from my See, and that is very long. The affairs of the diocese rest anxiously upon me. I will ask you to send
a trusted man onward tonight, on your swiftest hobbie, to find
my vicar general at Rosscarbery, and bring him to meet me tomorrow on the way, and render account of his stewardship. And,
moreover, I have with me day and night the great responsibility
of this peerless relic, this miracle of heavenly favor to us of Ross.
I cannot be idling on the road till that is suitably bestowed in
my cathedral. I will have you bear me company, Turlogh, son of
Fineen. You are by repute well known to me, and you are of my
blood. We O'Mahonys of Muskerry are better sons of the church,
I fear, than you men here on the wild coast. Many evil tales reach
men's ears of deeds ill done here, in this rude Ivehagh. But you
yourself have borne always a name for piety and docility and
some little layman's learning. It was for this that I chose to make
my landing here and let Dunbeekin shelter the blessed relic first
of all in Ireland. Besides, there were strange ships to be seen off
Brookhaven and the Cape, which in these lawless waters might
signify nothing friendly. Has the country been more quiet and
better ordered in these later times?"

"It has never been more undisturbed than at this moment,"
replied Turlogh, stealing another furtive glance backward at the
priests. They smiled grimly at him and nodded their heads.

The bishop had closed his eyes, and his head drooped again

upon his breast. Thus he passed unheeding through the broken postern and saw nothing of the blackened havoc inside, where once the pleasant grassy bawn had been.

In the castle, urgent shift had been made to render certain lower rooms once more habitable. The bishop, when the tired men placed him upon the chair drawn forth with cushions by his servants, lacked the will to look about him. Turlogh, standing behind those who bore the lights, gazed, marveling, at the huge girth of the man, whose trunk strained to bursting the black robe with purple buttons in which it was encased. The swollen face, hanging in the shadow, was more a death's head than ever. Still he held the casket upon his knees. The priest signed to Turlogh to go out, and he did so. When he sent his physician to them, they more curtly bade him also to leave them.

When tomorrow came, no one in Dunbeekin found it strange that the bishop did not set forth on his journey. The most simple had seen death writ large upon him. The story that he knew nothing of the terrible devastation that had swept the land bare passed vaguely from mouth to mouth. It was not easy to understand that so lofty and pious an ecclesiastic, standing at the head of all men in the South for learning, should be in darkness in this matter, which was known to the very horse-boys. They dwelt curiously upon the thought of him—the high prelate with the marvelous relic, coming to shattered and spoilt Dunbeekin to die, and never seeing the ruin about him, never learning that his cathedral was destroyed, his palace in ashes, his vicar general hanged in the Bandon forest, his priests and people dispersed. It was all very strange and troubling to the mind.

After midday Turlogh went again, and the priests brought him into the presence of the bishop. Their faces had taken on a new fright, and they spoke in scared whispers as they moved along beside him.

"We know not how to tell him," they said. "He does be dying, and he will not listen. His confessor strove to speak to him of his end, but he drove him out with harsh words. At any hour the change may fall like a stroke upon him, and he not prepared! The crime of it would be resting like a mountain on our souls."

Turlogh would not promise to speak, but when he stood alone before Lawrence, son of Ivar, who still sat bolstered in his chair, still with the jeweled casket on his shapeless knees, the courage came to him.

"My lord," he said, "you are not better. My physician has no more than laid an eye on you, yet shakes his head and speaks gravely. Will you not be having your chaplain come to you?"

The bishop lifted his eyes, and they gazed sharply forth from the dulled, misshapen visage at his host. Minutes of silence passed thus.

"These frocked cowards of mine," he said at last, "they will have prompted you to this."

"They see what all see," replied the other. "It is high time for you to take thought of your peace with God and gain your victory for the example of lesser people."

The bishop's scrutiny of his kinsman's face was not relaxed, but the little eyes seemed to twinkle now, and a fugitive smile passed over the shaven, bloated jowl.

"I will not suffer my priests to be dictating to me," he said. "They have never dared give the law to me, living; it is not for them to be appointing a time for my death. I will choose my own season and the hour that pleases me best. St. Kiernan's bones! Am I less the bishop than I was?"

Turlogh smiled a little in turn. "I would not be saying you are less in any respect whatever," he replied. He stole a glance over the other's unwieldy bulk to point his meaning, and the bishop laughed painfully.

"You are more after my heart than the others," he sighed, "and I come to you at the end, only for burial at your hands. That is the way of life, Turlogh, son of Fineen, and the way of death, too. They speak a true word enough, these young men of mine. I cannot be going any further. I know it well enough that I shall die here in Dunbeekin. But it is not for them to tell me so. I was vicar general for twenty years, and lord bishop for eight, and no priest yet wagged his head before me or gave me the word what I was to do. They are not much, these striplings of mine. They stand in good subjection to me, but they have no invention in their minds. They would not be fit to bury a bishop. It should be a great spectacle, with armed men and fires and a blaze of jewels among the funeral hangings, and the keening of trained women in companies, so that children would remember it when they were palsied with old age. These trivial boys I have with me are not capable of it. They would not lay out the worth of ten cows on me. They have pure hearts but no proper sense of pageantry. Would *you* have been seeing any great prelate buried?"

Turlogh shook his head.

"But you have some learning," pursued the other. "It is known to you from books what princes and chieftains have done before our time to honor Holy Church. All they did I will be having done for me, and more, too. Some bishops there were who, in their last days, laid down their crosiers and put on the monk's habit, and died on the ashes in what they called humility. I am not one to crawl into heaven that way. I will be borne across my diocese with pomp, and the clashing of spears and shields about me; and I will be entering Rosscarbery with my bells tolling and my priests chanting as they walk two by two, and all the people wailing at the sides of the path—and kneeling, mind you, as I pass on my way, with this great relic still in my hands. And this is what you will do for me—and you will provide entertainment and good places for the bards and those who write chronicles in the abbeys, so that my fame may not suffer for the want of a supper or a stool by the fire, and you will administer my will and my estate as I devise. I ask you to promise me these things, Turlogh, son of Fineen, and you will swear it with your hand on this casket."

The old chief's eyes shone with a prompt and welcome resolve. He laid his hand, above the bishop's, on the casing of the relic, and, kneeling to kiss the ring again, swore his oath.

"Send to me now my people," the prelate said, closing his eyes in weariness.

To the priests who came when his host had departed he gave commands. His *ordo*[7] should be brought to him, and parchment or paper for writing, and pens and ink, and thereafter no one of them, nor anybody save his oldest body-servant, should enter the room for the space of three days. When they told him, perforce, that the fire in the castle had swept away all writing materials, he fell into a rage, until they made shift with quills fresh-cut from a fowl dead in the bawn, and with a violet dye of wild cress compounded by the herb doctor. Then they left him alone with his *ordo*.

For three days he sat in solitude, and all were forbidden his presence. The old servant knew not save that he wrote for ever on the margins of his book, slowly and with sorry travail. He touched no food or drink in that time, and at night, still stretched half-seated in his chair, the casket upon his knees, he slumbered fitfully, eager always for the daylight and his writing again.

All Dunbeekin heard of these things and dwelt in thought on nothing else. It was in no man's mind to set one stone on another in repair of the ruin the English had wrought. No net was put into the bay, and the women lifted not a finger to the task of making curds and white meats. Cattle were killed, and

7. A guidebook for the clergy setting forth the important events for a given liturgical year and affording information regarding ritual norms for feast days and so forth. The bishop in the present circumstances would be keen to consult the book's material regarding funeral masses and the protocols surrounding a bishop's funeral. He writes the specific instructions for his own funeral in the book's margins.

their flesh seethed in new milk, for food, but no cake was baked. The strong meat put a stormy heart into the men. They ground their spearheads and javelins upon the stones, and cut from the green hides of the slain cattle new covers, soaked and stretched in sea brine, for their round shields. When they looked one into another's face, a flash of expectant eyes passed, like a beam of sunlight on a skene.[8] Their words were few, though, for the bishop had a great name in all Carbery, and the shadow of his passing laid a spell upon their tongues.

On the third day, a little after sunrise, a commotion stirred among the priests and the strangers of the prelate's household. The chaplain had been summoned to the room of death, and the bishop was making his confession. Then doors were opened, and Turlogh with those nearest him went in, until the chamber was filled, and the passage thronged with men lifting themselves on their toes to know what was to happen.

The bishop, still in his chair, stared out of his eyes helplessly and drew breaths which fought their way in and out of his vast girth of trunk. The mask which was his face was ashen- grey. The casket had been lifted from his knees, and a priest held it beside him, so that his ringed hand might lie upon it. The physician, bending on the other side, offered to loosen the robe drawn with oppressive tightness across his breast.

The bishop snarled an inarticulate dissent, and strove to lift his free hand.

"Not any button!" he murmured, thickly. "I abate no atom of my dignity. I will be dying with my robe seemingly disposed."

His eyes mounted above the pain to look at Turlogh.

"In my *ordo*," he gasped out laboriously, "all directions are there. You will observe the least of them!"

The lord of Dunbeekin bowed and made to take the book from the hand of the priest who held it. The bishop interposed

8. A knife or dagger.

with a hoarse call and strove to shake his head. Those closest round about gazed wonderingly into his troubled, frowning face to catch a hint of his meaning. The chaplain, bearing the viaticum, stooped forward to listen for some whispered words.

"Open the book!" the slow, difficult command came. "Search the rubric. Read aloud to me in what manner a bishop receives the viaticum!"

The priest with the book fumbled at its pages. He turned pale as he did so and cast a confused, appealing glance at the chaplain. He went on, moving the leaves aimlessly, with a hanging lip.

"Read, read!" insisted the bishop in stern monition.

The priest had the passage before him. He was a young man, soft-faced and gentle of mien. The tears started in his eyes, and his mouth quivered as he remained speechless.

The bishop sought to rise in his chair. His lifeless face drew itself into lines of wrath; his eyes gleamed, and his voice gurgled turbulently in his throat for a moment, then burst forth in loud, unnatural tones.

"Shrine of Fachnan![9] Will you not be reading? Read aloud the words! In precisely what manner will a bishop, in the hour of death, receive the body of our Lord? I command you to read it!"

In terror-stricken lispings the priest mumbled from the book shaking under his eyes that the bishop should kneel to receive the Host.

Lawrence, son of Ivar, raised his arms a little.

"Lift me then to my knees," he ordered them, with authority. They cried out at him in frightened entreaty: "For Christ sake!" the chaplain, foremost among them, pleaded. "You cannot kneel, my lord! I implore you! I have the power—I omit the kneeling."

The bishop bent his brows angrily upon his confessor and shook his arms upward again with an imperious gesture.

9. St. Fachnan, first bishop of Ross. He founded a school and monastery in Cork in the sixth century.

"You have power, have you!" he called out in truculent scorn. "You will be giving the law to me, will you? Am I your bishop? Tell me that, you cropped clown! And will you stand between God's anointed and the rubric? Here you, Gilcrest! You, Duarcan! Lift me to my knees! I command it! I'll be dying as befits my rank and my station!"

Tremblingly the two servants moved to his side, and, with shoulders under his arms, raised the bishop to his full height. Then they bent to lower him forward. The clerics had turned their brimming eyes away. Turlogh, and the armed men of his sept behind him, who were unafraid yet looked to see a countenance desolated by an anguish too great to gaze upon, beheld instead a strange luminous softness spread over the bishop's swollen lineaments, and bring them back to human likeness, and stamp upon them the aspect of triumphant martyrdom. The face of the bishop was white as death now, and as he sank slowly to his knees, drops of water stood upon his brow. But a light of peace subdued all torment in his calm eyes.

Thus Lawrence, son of Ivar, gained victory of pilgrimage and devotion and penance. He seemed to the kneeling throng that filled the room to draw no breath, as the tremulous chaplain, bending down, anointed him for his entrance into the company of the saints. While the words of absolution quivered upon the lips of the ministrant, the bishop fell forward upon his face.

"A spirit of pure chastity has departed from among us," said Turlogh solemnly blessing himself as he rose to his feet.

"A tower of magnanimity and a treasury of wisdom in these parts," responded the confessor.

"A bestower of rich presents and a chief conservator of the canons of the church," added one of the priests.

The sound of the women's lamentations without came into the chamber of death. Turlogh put his hand upon his sword, and drew it forth, and kissed the cross upon its hilt.

"His lightest wish for his burial will be a law to me and to the people of my house." He spoke the words slowly, and his armed men, hearing them, lifted their heads in the air.

III

In the noon hour Dunbeekin stood again under the gray sky, deserted and soundless. Old Turlogh, girt as no man had seen him before, with iron upon his breast and a cap of shining steel drawn over his whitened locks, had gathered all who belonged to him in the bawn, and spoken to them from where he stood on the stone of the broken well.

"I will be going hence," he said, "to bury the holy man, my kinsman, my lord bishop. His commands rest upon me, and they are welcome. No other such honor has befallen to me in all my years. But honors that have no substance to the touch are not alike in all eyes. Moreover, this transparent gem of pure piety whom I will be laying in his appointed grave was not close in blood to us. His people have our name, and they are Kian's sons as well as we, but their birthplace is strange to us. In Muscarry of the Rushes they do not be giving us of the coast much praise and affection. It is their custom to speak of us as pirates and heathens, and even he who lies dead within was not slow to utter the same word. The saint of his vows, too, the holy maiden of the O'Driscoll's—*Mughain*—is no friend to us of Ivehagh.[10] Our sea forts are spattered with the blood of the O'Driscoll's, and my great father, Fineen, son of Conogher of the steeds, broke down their shrine of Mughain at Dunashad. Therefore you are not bound by any near tie to give your lives for this burial. I will not be laying it on any man for his duty that he should come with me. Those with minds to the contrary will be freely returning now to the hills, for their greater safety, and holding this place till my brother comes

10. An ancient saint of various mythic personas and place associations. See O'Riain, *A Dictionary of Irish Saints*.

back from the army of the Earl. I will be taking with me none but willing people, and I will have it known to them that they are not like to see Dunbeekin again with any mortal vision."

When Turlogh in another hour led forth from his gates the funeral train of the bishop, no breathing creature remained behind. There went with him, to the last one, the robed men of his household, and his galloglasses and kerns, and the hooded women of years, who struck their hands together and screamed the death-wail as they walked; and the younger maidens with short veils, and even to the smallest of the children, clinging to their mothers' skirts. And the spade- men and horse-boys drove forward and led the horses not bearing riders, and on these were fastened all the chattels and light possessions of Dunbeekin. In the center of the armed men walked the priests, and before them proceeded eight servants, bearing upon sticks the pall of the bishop; and all could see him lying there, under a seemly cover of black cloth, with the casket of the holy relic rising sharp-cornered above his breast.

There was no heat in the air, and they moved on over the wasted country at a good speed. As twilight gathered, they passed from the defiles of the hills into greener vales, where the streams ran eastward and no marks of ruin met the eye. Here the beasts fed upon the harvest grass, while a heifer was slain and seethed for human eating; and here the fighting men looked a last time to their blades and spearheads and their yew bows. Darkness fell, and they went forward again, with Goron the Quick-Eyed in front of all, calling the way, and the keening of the weary elder women rising no higher than the moan of the sea wind they had left behind forever. In the night, further inland, lights began to gleam upon their course, as if on beacon hills beyond. Then a small flame, borne swiftly, crossed the path nearer at hand. The pale overcast moonlight made visible only the dim rolling shape of the slope down which they were making their way.

Goron ran back, and then, after hasty whispers of counsel, went forth into the darkness, with his hand on Turlogh's bridle rein. They were well in advance of the train when the light they had seen and then lost flashed again suddenly in their very faces; and they, halting, beheld crowded black shadows of men straight in their path.

"What is all this? Who are you?" was sharply demanded out of the obscurity, in a tongue strange to Goron.

Turlogh, the learned man, had the English.

"I am the lord of Dunbeekin," he made answer, in a cool voice, "and I will be proceeding with my people to Rosscarbery to bury our lord bishop, as befits his station and great fame in these parts."

The voice of the unseen captain laughed, amid a sinister rattle of steel on steel.

"There is no Rosscarbery left on the face of the earth. There is no bishop, alive or dead. There is no lord of Dunbeekin but only an old thief of a rebel hiding in the mountains, who called himself such among his native savages. Him we will hang when found, as we hung his kinsman, the barbarian Donal *Grany*, on the lintel of his own castle in Kinalmeaky."

"I am he of whom you speak," returned Turlogh; "and when I have buried my bishop, and fulfilled to the last the commands of his testament, which I have here with me writ by his own hand, we will talk further of this hanging. But now I will be moving forward on my way."

Other sounds of laughter rose about them in the darkness.

"They are all mere Irish," said a rough man's voice, after a moment.[11] "They bear with them a bier of some sort, true enough, but they have their women and children and herds with them as

11. "Mere" here, though uncomplimentary, is not used in the dismissive sense the word now has, but in the old meaning of pure or unadulterated (i.e., these Irish are of the pure, unassimilated sort—Old Irish, Gaelic Irish).

well. It is a strange game. Why should we not fall upon them now, before they have wrought the mischief of their conceit?"

"You are outside the law," spoke the first voice, that of authority. "We may put you all to the sword, here where we find you."

"I know of no law but my lord bishop's wish," replied Turlogh. "I am not outside that. I will be making a truce with you until he has been buried as he desired. Thereafter I ask no accommodation at your hands."

"Saw anyone ever such another land of holy men and lunatics?" communed the English captain with the blackness.

"Nay," one of his party urged, "it is not holiness but empty superstition, and to be a lunatic argues previous sound wit, which these savages never yet possessed. Say rather an island of idolatrous idiots."

The captain spoke again: "If you are Turlogh Mahowne, as you declare yourself, go forward then to Rosscarbery, if you can find it by the smoke over its ashes, and bury your papist carrion wherever the ground is not baked too stiff for digging, and when you have made an end of it, then we will have more talk."

The day dawned and showed to Turlogh and his caravan bodies of armed men on either side, moving along at a distance, in even progress with the funeral train. There were leaders in the saddle, encased in metal to the thighs; and footmen, breached in buff leather and with iron caps, bore long pikes on their shoulders. In numbers they were to the men of Dunbeekin as three to one; and in another four hours, upon the meeting of the high roads outside Rosscarbery, two score more joined them.

"They are fine men," said Goron, walking at his master's bridle. "I have never seen them in the open country before. They are better than we are. They will make but one bite of us, as a white trout with the mayfly."

"The mayfly!" answered Turlogh musingly. "Two years does it be spending underground, preparing its wings. And then the portion of one day up above in the air and the sunlight, and it ends in the beak of a bird or the jaws of a strong fish. Your speech is always wise, Goran, son of Tiarnan. It is I who am the mayfly, and this is my one little morning in the world."

Where Rosscarbery had been, Turlogh and his people traced, through choked paths and streets blocked with stones of broken houses, the place of the cathedral. They moved about among its blackened ruins and, lifting great blocks of masonry from the site of the high altar, dug there a grave and shaped a rude coffin of large stones, and laid Lawrence, son of Ivar, to his rest. They knelt uncovered while the chaplain said the funeral mass; and the singing priests chanted, and the elder women raised their voices in a last wail over the grave.

Then Turlogh gave a sign to his people and, going out, led in his own horse over the tumbled debris of the shattered transept. He drew his sword, and the animal fell with a pierced throat upon the place where they had buried the bishop. The men of Dunbeekin brought forward the other horses, neighing in their fright, and slew them one by one; and the cattle, driven in and leaping wildly in terror over the despoiled floors, were beaten down with the war axes and piled, smoking, on the high altar. At Turlogh's command, the jewels and fine cloths and books they had brought were heaped here, too, and with his own hand he struck a flame and set them alight. The smoke curled thickly outward and forced the chieftain back. He led the way forth to the open air. In the space beyond the west front he came upon a line of English drawn close to bar his passage. Over his shoulders he saw other lines guarding the sides against escape. His eyes sought out the captain, and he moved toward him.

"There will be a price on my head?" he asked, calmly—"on me, Turlogh, son of the Fineen, lord in Dunbeekin?"

The other shook his head. "You flatter yourself," he said, "you were not accounted of sufficient dignity for that. A trifle of drink money, perhaps, to the man who should run you down in the bog and cut your throat: no more."

"That is very bad news for me," replied Turlogh. "If it were otherwise, I would be asking you for that money, to place it there in the fire I have built in offering to my lord bishop. All that I had I have given, but it is not nearly enough. My lord bishop was mercifully spared the knowledge of the ruin and great calamities that have fallen upon us all. He died bequeathing large monies to the poor, and the sum of the value of sixty cows for masses for his soul; and other sums for a grand tomb, and for needy scholars and the like; and I am pledged to carry out his will. His poor have been starved or murdered; his students are dispersed; out of charity the masses will be said in Spain and France and other pious lands whither our priests have fled. But I would not that any penny should be spared to the enrichment of his tomb. Yet if there be nothing more forthcoming, then there is an end to my task. And now my truce with you will be over, too."

The young Englishman looked at the tall pale old man in doubtful silence for a little.

"You are no better than a heathen in your spiritual part," he said at last; "but I know not that you are a harmful rebel. Get you back to your Dunbeekin, as you call it, and take your motley ragamen with you, and swear an oath of loyal behavior to Her Most Splendid Majesty before you go; and the truce—who shall say—it may last your lifetime. At the worst, it was your brother we wanted, not you."

Turlogh straightened his thin form, and stepped out to face the captain.

"They call me Turlogh of the Two Minds," he said, with a greater calmness than before. "All my life I have not shed any man's blood, because it did not seem to me to be wholly a good thing to do, and I hesitated. But now, in my old age, my last day, I have only one mind in me. You and your people have come where no one asked you, and you have put massacre and desolation of famine and destruction upon us, when we had not deserved it. And I have told you that our truce is ended, and you will not be believing it, and now I will prove it to you."

Upon the word he smote the captain in the face with one hand, and with the other he plunged his skene into his neck. The two men clutched each other, and as they toppled, writhing, to the ground, rival cries of battle split the air. The English, with full-mouthed oaths and shouts of wrath, hurled themselves forward. The Irish, huddling backward to guard their unarmed folk, raised a defiant answering yell and fought in wild despair. They were hewn down where they stood, and after them their priests and women and children. Nothing that had come out of Dunbeekin was left with a breath in it.

The English captain, chalk-faced and with his throat swathed in stained bandages, leaned upon his sword while the straps of his cuirass were unbuckled and the cumbrous breastplate lifted from him. He looked down with a rueful, musing half-smile at the trampled form of an old man which had been dragged out from a confused pile of bodies and lay stretched at his feet. The head was bruised and the white hair was torn and clotted, but the withered, upturned face, looking very small and waxen now, wore an aspect of pride and sweetness which moved him. He gently pushed the hair aside from the marble temples with his boot and sighed as he looked again.

"Shall we send the head to Cork?" asked another officer, resting on one knee beside the body. "After all, he was a lord in the eyes of the Irish, and he had a castle, such as it was."

"No," responded the captain, on reflection. "He came a long way to bury his bishop, and he gave him a funeral of distinction to the full measure of his ability. Bear him inside, and let him lie beside his bishop. They have heads to spare in Cork without his."

Then after a little pause he lifted his gaze and turned away.

"It may be that you are right," he said again. "It may be they are idolatrous idiots and nothing better, but when I looked upon the old man lying there, the whimsy came to me. I should have liked him to have been my father."

A sharp exclamation of surprise came from the kneeling officer, and the captain wheeled on his heel.

"I'll be sworn I saw it!" the former cried, staring fixedly down on the face on the ground. "When you spoke those words, the old rebel's body stirred, and his death's head shook itself."

The speaker had a knife out from his belt, and the captain bent to lay a sharply restraining hand on his arm. Together they scrutinized the body before them. It was plainly a corpse.

"My oath on it, he moved!" insisted the kneeling man.

"You dream!" said the captain, stoutly enough, but a little shudder ran through the sigh with which he turned away.

CHRONOLOGY

1538   Henry VIII excommunicated by the pope.

1541   Henry VIII declares himself King of Ireland.

1550   December 25, young Turlogh becomes chieftain of the Dunbeekin O'Mahonys in "In the Shadow of Gabriel."

1556   Plantation (Irish land seized and granted to foreigners) commences broadly.

1558   Reign of Queen Elizabeth begins (1558–1603).

1568   Munster: First Desmond Rebellion.

1579   Advance parties of Spanish army representing the pope arrive and prepare along southwest Irish coast for landing in Kerry. Setting for events in "The Path of Murtogh."

1580   Papal army ("The Path of Murtogh") defeated at Smerwick in Kerry. Edmund Spenser takes up residence in Cork.

1582   Tiege O'Mahony becomes chieftain in Ballydevlin in "The Wooing of Teige."

1594   Nine Years' War (1594–1603) begins.

1599   English army of some seventeen thousand under Sir Robert Devereux invades Ireland.

1601   Historic Defeat of Irish and Spanish armies by Mountjoy at Kinsale marks the conquest of Gaelic Ireland.

1602–3   British armies moving west from Kinsale defeat last remnants of Irish resistance in West Cork. Setting of "Truce of the Bishop."

1847–48   The Great Famine. West Cork is one of the hardest-hit areas.

CHRONOLOGY

1856	Harold Frederic born in Utica, New York.
1875 c.	Setting for "The Lady of Muirisc."
1879	April: Michael Davitt founds the Land League in Mayo. It becomes the National Land League.
1879 to mid-1880s	Dire food shortages in Western Ireland. Setting of "The Martyrdom of Maev."
1884	Frederic becomes London correspondent for *New York Times*.
1886	Gladstone commits Liberal Party to Irish home rule.
1890	Frederic's friend Tim Healy withdraws his support of Parnell, leads opposition.
1891	Parnell dies in October.
1893	Second Gladstone Home Rule bill rejected by Parliament. Frederic's *The Damnation of Theron Ware* is published.
1898	Harold Frederic dies of stroke.

BIBLIOGRAPHY

Bagwell, Richard. *Ireland under the Tudors*. 2 vols. London: Longman, 1885.

Bennett, Bridget. *The Damnation of Harold Frederic: His Lives and Works*. Syracuse: Syracuse University Press, 1997.

Berleth, Richard. *The Twilight of the Lords: Elizabeth I and the Plunder of Ireland*. New York: Rinehart, 2002.

Butler, F. T. *Gleanings from Irish History*. London: 1925.

Brigden, Susan. *New Worlds, Lost Worlds: The Rule of the Tudors, 1485– 1603*. New York: Penguin, 2000.

Campbell, Christy. *Fenian Fire*. New York: Harper, 2003.

Campbell, Joseph. *The Poems of Joseph Campbell*. Dublin: Figgis, 1963.

Callanan, Frank. *T. M. Healy*. Cork: Cork University Press, 1996.

Cather, Willa. *The World and the Parish: Willa Cather's Articles and Reviews 1893–1902*. Vol. 2. Edited by William M. Curtin. Lincoln: University of Nebraska Press, 1970.

Connolly, S. J., ed. *The Oxford Companion to Irish History*. Oxford: Oxford University Press, 1998.

———. *Making Ireland British, 1500–1650*. New York: Oxford University Press, 2003.

———. *Contested Island: Ireland, 1460–1630*. London: Oxford University Press, 2007.

———. *Divided Kingdom: Ireland, 1630–1899*. New York: Oxford University Press, 2008.

Crane, Stephen. *Crane: Prose and Poetry*. New York: Library of America, 1996.

Dickson, David. *Old World Colony: Cork and South Munster 1630–1830*. Madison: University of Wisconsin Press, 2005.

Dinesen, Isak. "The Deluge at Norderney." In *Seven Gothic Tales*. New York: Vintage: 1991.

"Dinner to Mr. Harold Frederic." *New York Times*, June 29, 1886.

Edwards, David, Padraig Lenihan, and Clodagh Tait, eds. *Age of Atrocity: Violence and Political Conflict in Early Modern Ireland*. Dublin: Four Courts, 2010.

BIBLIOGRAPHY

Ellis, Peter Berresford. *Eyewitness to Irish History*. Hoboken N.J.: Wiley, 2004.

Falls, Cyril. *Elizabeth's Irish Wars*. Syracuse, N.Y.: Syracuse University Press, 1997.

Ferraro, Thomas J. "Of 'Lascivious Mysticism' and Other Hibernian Matters." *U.S. Catholic Historian* 23, no. 3 (Summer 2005): 17.

Foster, R. F. *Modern Ireland, 1600–1972*. London: Penguin Group, 1988.

Franchere, Hoyt C., and Thomas F. O'Donnell. *Harold Frederic*. New York: Twayne, 1961.

Frederic, Harold. "London's Budget of News." *New York Times*, February 15, 1885.

———. "The Martyrdom of Maev." *New York Ledger*, March 22, 1890, 1–3; March 29, 1890, 3.

———. *The Return of the O'Mahony*. New York: Dillingham, 1892.

———. "The Ireland of Today." *Fortnightly Review* LX (November 1893).

———. "The Rhetoricians of Ireland (over the signature "X")." *Fortnightly Review* 60 (December 1, 1893).

———. "The Path of Murtogh." *Idler*, May 1895, 455–79.

———. "In the Shadow of Gabriel." *Black and White*, December 25, 1895, 21–26.

———. "The Truce of the Bishop." *Yellow Book*, Oct 7, 1895, 84–111.

———. "The Coast of White Foam." *New York Times Magazine*, November 1, 1896, 4.

———. "The Wooing of Teige." *Pall Mall Magazine*, November 10, 1896, 418–26.

———. "Letter to James N. Dunn." In *The Correspondence of Harold Frederic*. The Harold Frederic Edition, vol. 1. Fort Worth: Texas Christian University Press, 1977.

———. *The Damnation of Theron Ware*. New York: Penguin, 1986.

Garner, Stanton. "Some Notes on Harold Frederic in Ireland," *American Literature* 39, no. 1 (March 1967): 60–74.

———. "More Notes on Harold Frederic in Ireland." *American Literature* 39, no. 4 (January 1968): 560–562.

———. *Harold Frederic*. Minneapolis: University of Minnesota Press, 1969.

Haines, Paul. "Harold Frederic." PhD dissertation. New York University, New York, N.Y., 1945.

Harris, Frank. "Harold Frederic Ad Memoriam." *Saturday Review of Politics, Literature, Science, and Art* LXXXVI, no. 527 (October 22, 1898).

Healy, T. M. *Letters and Leaders of My Day*. 2 vols. London: Butterworth, 1929.

158

Jeffares, A. N. *A New Commentary on the Poems of W. B. Yeats.* London: Macmillan, 1984.

Jefferies, Henry A. *The Irish Church and the Tudor Reformations.* Dublin: Four Courts, 2010.

Keating, Geoffrey. *The History of Ireland from the Earliest Period to the English Invasion.* Translated by John O'Mahony. New York: Haverty, 1857.

Klopfenstein, Glenn D. "'The Flying Dutchman of American Literature': Harold Frederic and the American Canon, a Centenary Overview." *American Literary Realism* 30, no. 1 (Fall 1997): 34–46.

Leerssen, Joep. *Mere Irish and Fior-Ghael: Studies in the Idea of Irish Nationality, its Development and Literary Expression prior to the Nineteenth Century.* Notre Dame, Ind.: Notre Dame University Press, 1997.

Lennon, Colm. *Sixteenth Century Ireland: The Incomplete Conquest.* Dublin: Gill, 2005.

Maume, Patrick. *The Long Gestation: Irish Nationalist Life 1891–1918.* New York: St. Martin's Press, 1999.

Moody, T. W., and F. J. Byrne. *A New History of Ireland, Vol. 3: Early Modern Ireland 1534–1691.* Oxford: Oxford University Press, 1993.

Myer, G. J. *The Tudors: The Complete Story of England's Most Notorious Dynasty.* New York: Bantam, 2011.

Myers, Robert M. *Reluctant Expatriate: The Life of Harold Frederic.* Westport, Conn.: Greenwood, 1995.

Noble, Allen G. *An Ethnic Geography of Utica, New York.* Lewiston N.Y.: The Edwin Mellen Press, 1999.

Oates, Joyce Carol. "Rediscovering Harold Frederic." *New York Times Book Review*, December 17, 1995.

O'Connor, Frank. *The Big Fellow.* Dublin: Poolbeg, [1937] 1979.

O'Curry, Eugene. *On the Manners and Customs of the Ancient Irish.* Dublin: 1873.

O'Donnell, Thomas F. "Harold Frederic (1856–1898)." *American Literary Realism* 1 (1967): 39–44.

O'Flaherty, Liam. *The Life of Tim Healy.* New York: Harcourt, 1927.

Ohlmeyer, Jane. *Making Ireland English: The Irish Aristocracy in the 17th Century.* New Haven, Conn.: Yale University Press, 2012.

O'Mahony, Edward. "West Cork and the Elizabethan Wars." http://www.geocities.ws/eomahony/Elizabethan.htm.

———. "Timothy Michael Healy: Politician and First governor-General of the Irish Free State." http://www.geocities.ws/eomahony/Healy.htm.

BIBLIOGRAPHY

O'Mahony, John (Rev.). *History of the O'Mahony Septs of Kinelmeky and Ivagha*. Cork, 1913.

Ò Riain, Pádraig. *A Dictionary of Irish Saints*. Dublin: Four Courts, 2011.

O'Riordan, Michelle. *The Gaelic Mind and the Collapse of the Gaelic World*. Cork, Cork University Press, 1990.

Osborne, Sidney Godolphin. *Gleanings in the West of Ireland*. London, 1850.

O'Sullivan, Leanne. "On the Beara Peninsula: Written in Stone." *New Hibernia Review* 17, no. 3 (Autumn 2013): 9–14.

Otway, Caesar. *Sketches in Ireland: Descriptive of Interesting, and Hitherto Unnoticed Districts, in the North and South*. Edinburgh, 1827.

Payne, Robert. *A Brief Description of Ireland*. London, 1590.

Plunkett, Horace. *Ireland in the New Century*. London: J. Murray, 1904.

Raleigh, John Henry. Introduction to Harold Frederic's *The Damnation of Theron Ware*. New York: Holt, 1967.

Spenser, Edmund. *A View of the Present State of Ireland*. Edited by Andrew Hadfield and Willy Maley. London: Blackwell, 1997.

Stafford, Thomas. *Pacata Hibernia, Ireland Appeased and Reduced: A History of the Wars of Ireland in the Reign of Queen Elizabeth*. London: 1821.

Stanhurst, Richard. *Great Deeds in Ireland: Richard Stanhurst's De Rebus in Hibernia Gestis*. Edited by John Barry and Hiram Morgan. Cork: Cork University Press, 2013.

Sugg, Richard. *Mummies, Cannibals and Vampires: The History of Corpse Medicine from the Renaissance to the Victorians*. New York: Routledge, 2011.

Tinniswood, Adrian. *Pirates of Barbary: Corsairs, Conquests, and Captivity in the 17th-Century Mediterranean*. New York: Penguin, 2010.

Trump, Miss. *Geraldine of Desmond, or, Ireland in the Reign of Elizabeth: An Historical Romance*. 3 vols. London, 1829.

Whitehead, Alfred North. *Science and the Modern World*. New York: Mentor, 1960.

Wilson, Edmund. "Harold Frederic: The Expanding Up-Stater." In *The Devils and Canon Barham*, 48–76. New York: Farrar, 1968.

Woodward, Robert H. "Harold Frederic: A Study of His Novels, Short Stories, and Plays." PhD dissertation, Indiana University, Bloomington, Ind., 1957.

Yeats, William Butler. *The Collected Poems of William Butler Yeats*. Edited by Richard J. Finneran. New York: Simon and Schuster, 1989.